Love, Loss and Lyonesse:
50 Cornish Poems

A.C Miles-Smith

I dedicate this book
with all my love
to my beautiful daughter Free…
my gallant son Will…
and my bold grandson Joe.

"Tis better to have loved and lost
than never to have loved at all."
"In Memoriam A.H.H."
By Alfred Lord Tennyson
1849

Introduction

A while ago I was browsing in a local bookshop and came across a copy of Seamus Heaney's book; '100 Poems'. I had written my first book 'Dandelions and Snails': an autobiography, in 2015, this contained both narrative and poems, and I had been considering creating a collection of purely poems for a while. So I set myself a challenge. I vowed that I would write a book of 101 poems.

I have always been interested in poetry and writing, and I have a degree in English Literature and Philosophy. However, writing a poetry book was harder than I ever imagined, and it took me two years to write 50 poems. In fact, writing my first book was much more straight forward for me, by comparison. Therefore, working on that premise, it will take me two more years to finish my aimed target of the antholgy of '101 poems'.

And here I must thank Jackie Curtis for all her patience and work in helping me to finish this publication.

I'm hoping that in this book of poetry of 'Love, Loss and Lyonesse', you will find poems that inspire, entertain, and amuse you; poems that will make you laugh; and poems that will make you cry.
(If my poems don't make you laugh or cry, maybe my sketches will).

Now seriously, above all, I hope the poems will instill a sense of Cornish pride within you, and will mould and strengthen your hearts, so you may become protectors of our mystical land.

Wishing You Well... Anna ...

Contents

Pre-Historic Cornwall

1. Snail Meditation: This time the snail comes first
2. Lanyon Quoit
3. Fern
4. Crow
5. Fairies of Madron Wishing Well
6. The Hawthorn Tree
7. St Michaels Mount

Years
400-600 AD

8. King Arthur and Excalibur

1600's

The English Civil War: The Battle at Stamford Hill, Bude

9. Before the Battle - 16th May 1643
10. After the Battle

1700's – 1800's

11. Mary Bryant: The Cornish Highway Woman of Fowey
12. Madron Workhouse
13. Good Night My Darling Bessie
14. Ding Dong Mine I
15. Ding Dong Mine II
16. The Ballad of Eliza Jane
17. The Cornish Wind
18. The Smugglers
19. Trengwainton
20. Cold Madron Day

The Fantasy Years

21. Ebb and Flow
22. The Gypsy Girl of Morvah Part 1
23. The Gypsy Girl of Morvah Part II

24. The Ghost of the Gypsy Girl of Morvah Part III
25. The Mermaid of Morvah
26. Mischievous Piskies
27. An April Awakening
28. The white Owl Angel - For Marjorie & Cathy

<u>1800's – 1900's</u>

29. The Improvisers - My poem for Alfred Wallis – Cornish Painter, 1855 – 1942
30. Fragments - My poem for Sven Berlin – Cornish Painter, Sculpture, Poet, Author, 1911 – 1999
31. Captain - My poem for Sydney Graham, Celtic Poet – Born in Scotland, moved to Cornwall, 1918 – 1986

<u>1930's – The approach of World War</u>

32. Which way is the wind blowing?

<u>1940's – The Battle of Britain – 1940, 10th July – 31st October</u>

33. Cheer Up Old Boy

<u>1944 – 6th June D Day</u>

34. The Place of No Sorrow

<u>1945 -Post War Cornwall</u>

35. Stillness
36. The Healing Has Begun
37. Destiny
38. Carbon to Carbon
39. Lamorna – The Woodcutters

<u>1950's – Early 60's - The Austerity Years</u>

40. The Tumbling Year
41. Sweetness
42. That Hot June Day
43. Fallow but not forgotten
44. René's Bridge

1960's - The Swinging Sixties

    45. The Sixties - For Diane & John
    46. The Blacksmith and the Ballerina

To Be In Harmony with Nature and the Universe

    47. Reynard the Fox
    48. Brock the Badger
    49. Boris The Buzzard
    50. Mythica

Notes

1. Lanyon Quoit
2. Fern
3. Crow
4. Fairies of Madron Wishing Well
5. The Hawthorn Tree
6. St Michael's Mount
7. King Arthur and Excalibur
8. The English Civil War
9. Mary Bryant
10. Madron Workhouse
11. Goodnight My Darling Bessie
12. Ding Dong Mine
13. The Ballad of Eliza Jane
14. Trengwainton House
15. 1800's - 1900's - These Three Cornish Painters
16. Cheer Up Old Boy
17. Carbon to Carbon and Lamorna - The Woodcutters
18. Reynard The Fox
19. Brock the Badger

Pre-Historic Cornwall

1. **Snail Meditation**

Shine snail
shine
your being
your total
all,
slimy
trail
shimmering
on
grey
granite
wall.

Swirl snail
swirl
be
subtle,
be
debonair,
in
dark brown
and
beige,
you
are always
here.

'Be' snail
be
bold
in your shell,
for your
secrets
are
not
yet to tell,
for you always
guard
your secrets
well.

Snail,
your silence
is your
power
so
ruminate
contemplate
cogitate
hour
by
hour
by
hour
by
hour.

Snails have lived on this planet for 150 million years.

2. **Lanyon Quoit**

The proud
dragon,
defiantly
stands,
calmly
surveying
his
panoramic
lands.

Eternal
and alone,
the harsh
rains of time,
have beat,
on this
granite
stone.

For many
moons and stars
have come
and gone,
and many
ships
have sailed,
and I
have
stood here
for

everyone,
my strength
has thus
prevailed.

Any many
feet
have pattered
past,
and many
golden
lights,
have shone
beneath my
pillars
on endless
summer
nights.

Sometimes
I whisper
on the
wind
for
hare and
fox
to hear,
and I
know
they keep

my council,
for my
teachings
are
austere.

And
if you too
listen
carefully,
then you
may
understand,
and
the world
will live
in peace
as our
creator
has planned.

*Note number 1.

Fern
Inna.
March 2020

3. Fern

We are
the
forest
fern
as here
our skeletons
show,
and
the soft
golden
swirls
of our
memories
around
us
grow
and grow.

Primordial
in
silence
we swirl
and swirl,
and
through
our spiritual
energy
we
gain
wisdom
of
the world.

In the
beginning

we saw
the sliding
serpent,
we smelt
the earthen
apple,
and
for seven
days we
hid
in darkness
while
God
and
the devil
did
battle.

We
saw
the compass
in
the sky,
we
felt
the granite
burst,
we heard
the
lowing
of the
beast,
for
we
were here
first.

We
saw
across
the cloudy
planet
the
dinosaur's
gigantic
frame,
reckless
roaring
rippling,
with
cruel
intentions
he
came.
Teeth
and claw
sharpened,
powerful tail
curling,
stomping
across
the land,
out of
the
mists
swirling.

In fear
and isolation
we crouched,
whispered
and

shivered,
were we
to be
devoured
in gulps,
or
from
these
vicious
jaws
be delivered?

We saw
Neolithic
woman
sitting
sewing
skins,
waiting
for
her
first child,
when
her time
begins.
The fire
burns
bright
and she
must
keep it
so,
to guard
against
wolf
and tiger
and other
barbaric
foe.

Then
as light
breaks
across
the tangled
hillside
to her
the hunt
returns,
across
the glowing
hillside
comes
the babe's
first
dawn.

We saw
the Romans
when
first
they invaded
in 55BC,
we saw
the
ancient Britons
and
how bravely
they
fought
to defend
their beloved
country.

We saw
Julius Caesar
and
his
treacherous
rivals,
as
they stood
in
circular
rounds,
assessing
their
survival.

And now
we ferns
stand
in
circular rounds
to talk,
debate
and meet,
and see
how
the bluebells
gather
below
in homage
at
our feet.
Like
Roman soldiers
they stand

and
listen
as
in
the sun
their
helmets
glisten.

Then in
AD793
the Vikings
came
across
the sea,
they came
to kill
to pillage
and
plunder,
behind
them rode
their
red headed
fiend,
THOR
Their God
Of
Thunder.

We saw
the fires
as they
burnt
our lands,
we heard
screams
wrought
by brutal
hands,
we curled
in silence
keeping
ourselves
small,
we curled
and hid
ourselves
from
the
thrall.

Now
we've told you
most of our,
story
so please
let us sleep,
in
the shady
lanes
where
fairies
peep,
and
where
on hawthorn
tree
and silver
birch,
small
starlings
and
ruby
robins
perch,
and mossy
granite
smells
so sweet,
and golden
celandine
shine
and meet.

Let
us rest
now
and regain
our strength,
for
you will
awaken
us again
at length.
Be it
marauding
tribes
or fire
or flood
or daggers
and knives
and
rivers
of blood,
or travellers
from
a different

time
and space,
who
visit,
destroy
then
leave
no trace.
Animal
or man,
Who
can
discern?
For
they will
all
acknowledge
the
humble
fern.

*Note number 2

4. Crow

Quwaa
Quwaa
Quwaa
the
black
crow
calls
while
on
thermals
of
warm
air
seagull
rises
and
falls.

Quwaa
Quwaa
Quwaa
sinister
crow
skulduggery
a-claw
victimised
scavengised
ostracized
as
outlaw.

Quwaa
Quwaa
Quwaa
suddenly
crow
is forgiven
and redeemed
and
given
more
a-crowlade
than
he could
ever
have dreamed.

*Note number 3

5.   The Fairies of Madron Wishing Well

In the hidden hall
of the fairy king
the golden fairies
dance and sing
on ethereal air
the fiddlers play
and soft silk curtains
swish and sway
and senses reel
under earths sweet bouquet
and mischievous fairies
hide and play

Tinkling sounds
from the great gold hall
serenade the fairies
with tunes celestial
green piskies prance
and swing and swirl
and silver bells
tinkle and toll.
Fairies fill their golden baskets
with fairy dew from heavens caskets
then bounce onto thermals
as waves of the sea
to surf to places
they need to be.

So close your eyes
and we'll bathe your lids
in enchanted words from old ballads
then come to help to sprinkle fairy dust
on yellow meadows and hawthorn bush
and come to adore
the sweet bluebell
in which our families
play and dwell
and heel toe down
to the Old Wishing Well.

Then beam away
to the jagged cliffs
where the pretty sea pink
laughs and lives
and blossoms above
the deep sea swell
to grace our days
with its pungent smell
yet return we will
when we hear the bell
for we are fairies
of the Wishing Well.

*.Note number 4

6. The Hawthorn Tree

The cold wind
has sent
us hither
the cold wind
has sent
us thither
and
in the
dizzy dance
of the
grey brown
spike,
we grow
whichever
way
we like,
now here
now there
now pointing
to
the cold
night air,
we are
dark
and sharp,
we are
silent
and wise
and nothing
escapes
our ancient
eyes.

And then
the Cornish
sun
appears
to drive
away
our inner
fears
to soothe
us gently
and in
that trance
our white
stars
blossom
with their
sweet
fragrance.

Then
t'is
time
to watch
and wait
while grow,
the yellow
gorse
at our
feet
below,
yet
still

with wisdom
we keep
our vow,
and as
the seagulls
follow
the farmer's
plough,
your
secrets
are
safe
in our
hawthorn
bough.

* Note number 5

7. St Michael's Mount

Some days are mystical as portals of time, and we should seize them and create a story or rhyme, and so I walk across the fields to write and sketch the Mount, and scribe a poem to chronicle the years that count.

And I ponder that thousands of years have passed, since the days of the ancient land of Lyonesse, and how around the Mount and under the seas, lie the remains of forests and the stumps of trees.

Time was then, time was when, the squirrel could jump across the trees, all the way from Penzance to the land of the Scillies.

And then the dreams and visions begin, and I am lost in the world of Nimue and Merlin, the world of Tristan Isolde, and romantic trysts, of lovers, jousts, and celtic mists.

Then through the mists of time, my mind falls upon, the shadow of the Giant, Cormoron.

His head
in his
hands,
his elbow
on his
knees,
he's
sitting
alone
above
the rocks,
and the
trees.

In olden
days
the Mount
was known,
as the
White Rock
In the
Wood,
and
giants
roamed
around
this land
seeking
Englishmen's
blood!

Yet
Cormoron
had
other
plans as
he loved

his high
top throne,
so he
built
a castle
to view
the land,
took a
wife Cormelia,
and
set up
home.

In that
flooded
forest,
behind
the salty
sea mists,
do these
souls
still dwell?
Do they
dream
of escaping
from the
deep sea
swell?
Or are
they
happy
in their
watery homes?
With the
fairies,
the pixies,
the unicorns

and gnomes.

Then
a beautiful
butterfly
flits
past my
eyes,
and
dances
in the
sunlit
skies,
and I
am
reminded
of our
fleeting
lives,
as
onto
his
sketched
outline
he dives,
he sits
cheekily
there,
as if
to say,
enough
of the
past,
what about
today?

Then he

tiptoes
around
on my
sketch
pad
and I
hear
the clipping
of his
tiny feet,
then he
carefully
returns
to his
pencilled
outline,
like he
wants
to remain
sweet
and neat.

On his
wings
and
his
'trompe
L'oeil'
eyes,
are the
colours
of deep
sea blue
and
coral
shell,
they
shine
as a
mermaid's
pretty
necklace,
from a
hidden
aqua
dell.

Oft
in my
childhood
dreams
I did
see,
a lion
emerging
from out
of the
sea,
bringing
a message
of truth
and
bravery.
Yet
this
butterfly
so fragile
and light,
had
brought
a similar
strong
message,
and
philosophical
insight.

And
then
he gently
flutters
away,
as if
to say,
concentrate
on your
work
today,
concentrate
on what
you know,
for that
was then
and this
is now.

* Notes numbers 6 and 7

Years
400 - 600 AD

8. King Arthur and Excalibur

King Arthur with Excalibur
did ride these windy moors
thundering
on hill and dale
across the land
from golden strand
to bay
of sea shelled shores.

Sunlight on steel
flashes
as over the land
he dashes
through shallow
stream
splashes
silver clinks
metal clashes.

He pulled
Excalibur
from the stone
he made
the kingdom
all his own
sent the evil
ones into
retreat
to lay
devotion
at his
lover's feet.

We too
can change
our destiny
with
the alchemy
of our dreams
we can set
in store
the mystery
of our
rich
bejewelled
seams.

And so
the journeyman
onward
he did
ride
on with Llamrei
his beloved
charger
and Excalibur
by his side

Past
Ding Dong
mine
and
Mount Whistle
past
humble weed

and
royal thistle.

See
how Arthur
dreams,
his eyes
fixed
on the
horizon
while
horses' hooves
and
heroes' heart
beat
in strong
unison.

Small birds
fly high
in startled
confusion
they shoot
from bush
scared by
the intrusion.
They swarm
and squawk
from
hideaways
and ditches
like handfuls
of seeds
thrown

from farmer's
old britches.

Now Carrion
crow
he calls
time
he knows
it's all
illusion,
has seen
it all
before
down centuries
of dark
confusion,
the black philosopher
of
self-illusion.

Crow watches
Arthur
and his
men
as he
has
watched
them
down through
passages
of time
and
knows
he could
easily follow

if so
inclined.

Yet
knowing
and
trusting
them
he lets
them pass;
sparkling
through the
woods
of Lyonesse.

For
today
crow
has
work
to do
alarms
to call
messages
to
construe.

And reaching
the cliffs
high above,
Arthur
sees Guinevere,
his world
his love.
Towards
her
he gallops,
in his
strong
arms
en-velopes.

Dancing
on moonbeams
comes
the fine
sea spray
and
tiny birds
sing
for the
closing
of the
day.

And
flying
across
the
darkening
strand,
crow
watches
the lovers
walk hand
in hand.

*Note numbers 7 and 6

1600's
The English Civil War:
The Battle at Stamford Hill, Bude

9. Before the Battle – 16ᵗʰ May 1643

The softest of whispers
pierced through my heart
when I heard your gentle voice say,
'My darling we must part.'

Through magic nights we have lain,
and I am glad to be your bride
but now the rolling drum beats loud,
and to battle you must stride.

You took the King's shilling,
so now you must go,
you have to be willing,
to slaughter the foe.

You took up the gun,
you took up the knife,
and now you must leave
your son and your wife.

I turn to your pillow,
a single rose in your place,
I turn to my child,
and touch his sweet face.

"Take up the fife,
take up the drum
but for God's sake don't take up
the knife and the gun."

*And the softest of whispers
still pierces my heart,
will the world still keep turning
while we are apart?*

*Note number 8

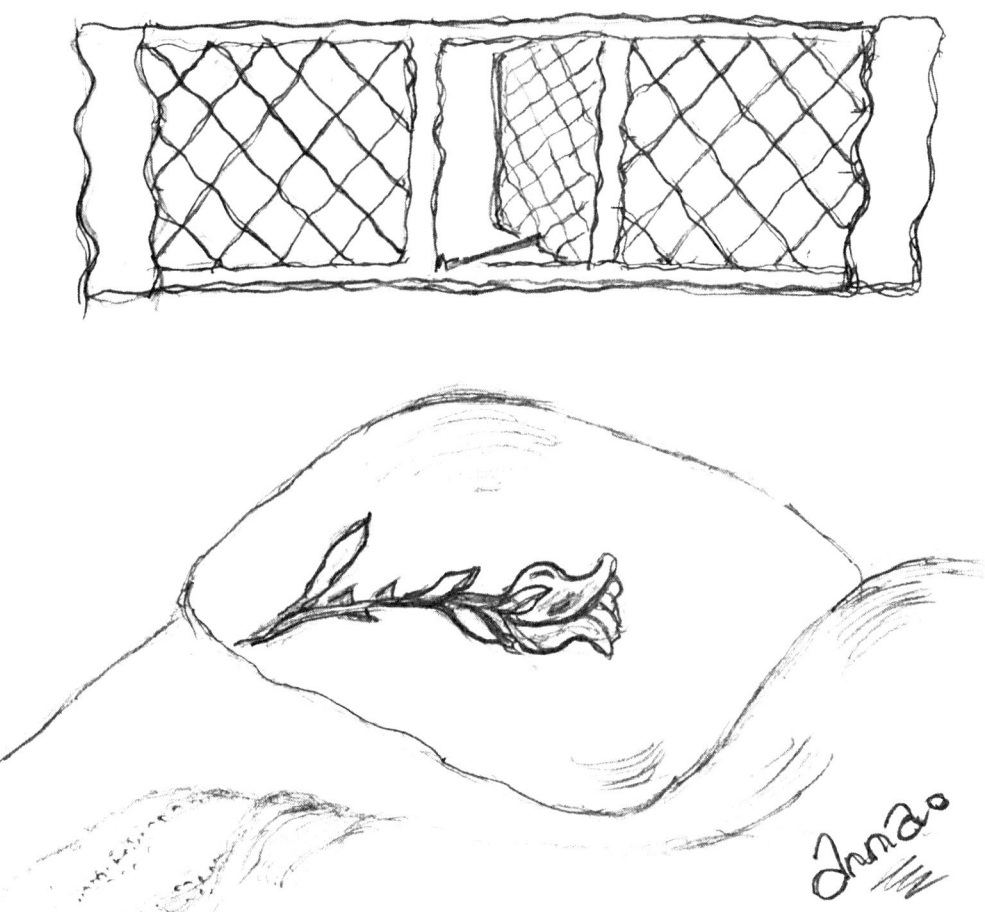

10. After the Battle: Drummer Boy

A
black night
a 'Blake'
sky,
dark
dark
navy blue
clouds
high,
leaked
from
the
ink pen
to splash
in
the eye,
of the
opal
full moon.

A
witches
night
of incantations,
crawl
through
smoke
hallucinations,
cauldron
cackle
fire
crackle,
platoon

of
vultures
post
battle.
Drummer Boy
of
red and gold
beat
the drum
for brave
and bold.
You
who have
survived
to tell,
of the
blood
the muskets
the noise
the smell.

Tread
bravely
Drummer
Boy
don't walk
on
the dead,
don't
walk
in their
footsteps
where

they
have tread,
return
to your
Mother
supper
and bed,
and shake
those memories
from
your
young
head.

"Mama
Mama
why
oh why
do
they lie
eyes
wide open
and gaze
at
the sky?
For them
not a
word?
Not
a tear?
Not
a kiss?

did
their
little
lives
amount
to this?"

"Son
they have
lain
that way
Since
time begun
and
they will
lie
that way
for
time
to come.

Not
until
we learn
to live
in peace
will
we
close
our eyes
and
find
release."

Mama
is papa
lying
there
with
those men?
Is that
why
he'll
never
be home
again?
"Did he
pick up
the knife
did he
pick up
the gun,
thinking
that
for King
and for
country
the
battle
could
be
won.

When he
took up
the knife
when he
took up
the gun
did he
not think
that his
family
might
become
undone?"

"Son,
he had
to leave
to fight
for the
crown,
he had
drunk
from the
tankard
into which
the
shilling
was
thrown.
He knew
the risks,
and my
poor heart
is broken,
and all
for the
sake
of the
King's
silver
token."

1700's - 1800's

11. Mary Bryant: The Cornish Highway woman of Fowey

The following poem is based on a true story. Mary was born into a fishing family in Fowey in 1765.

In 1765
on a sunny
May morn,
in the Cornish town
of Fowey
a little girl
was born.

Never did
her parents
realise
that her
life
would be
so fraught,
full of hardships
and danger,
worse
than
her parents
could ever
have thought.

And Mary
grew up strong
and fearless,
became a
highway woman
of great
renown,
and soon
the gossip
and the fear
quickly
spread
about the town.

And one day
on the Plymouth Road
she made
her biggest mistake,
when a silk bonnet
and ribbons
from a grand lady
Mary and her accomplices
did take.

And so
Mary and her
two friends
were condemned
to swing,
but at
the intangible
hour
before dawn
a pardon
they did bring.

Not to die
on the gallows,
not to swing
and sway,
but to spend
7 years penal
servitude
across the oceans
in
Botany Bay.

Now Mary's
Father
was a mariner
and had
taught
his daughter
well,
how to
fish
and how
to navigate
the perils
of the
deep sea swell.

And in May
of 1787
Mary had to
accept
her lot,
and was sent
to Australia
with the
'First Fleet'
on the cutter
the 'Charlotte'.

And while
on the way
to Botany Bay
Mary gave
birth to a
baby girl,
and we can
only wonder
how she
coped
bringing a baby
into her world.

Yet
when
they reached
Botany Bay
they suffered
immense hardships
and
great starvation
for Australia
was then
a harsh
and barren
nation.

Then
one man
stepped
up
to save them,

and
his name
was
Will Bryant,
he was
a clever
Cornish fisherman,
and on him
they became
reliant.

And Mary
fell in love
with Will
and together
they
set up home,
and soon
Will and Mary
had a
boy child
of their
very own.

You see
Will,
this clever
fisherman,
he knew
his seas
and his tides,
and together
they plotted
their escape
with their

two children
at their sides.

They
conspired together,
plotted
and planned,
struggled
and prayed,
to leave
that land.

And Will
was appointed
to manage
the colony's
fishing,
and so
could procure
anything
of his
wishing.

And Will
managed
to command
the Governor's
own cutter,
so for
their
plotted escape
what
could have
been better?

On 28th March
1791
they eventually
knew
their time
had come,
and
with baited
breath
on that eve
they waited
for
their time
to leave.

And as
silent
spirits
of the
night,
the brave band*
took
their
flight.

How had
they
managed
to procure
muskets
and ammunition
and
all necessities
for their
expedition?

How
had they
smuggled
food
for their
diet?
how had
they kept
their
children
quiet?
hidden
their muskets?
their
navigational
tools?
whispered
their plans
and stuck
to
their rules?

And
as
they
were
towed
out to sea
by locals
they
had befriended,

* 8 men 1 woman and 2 children

they wept
to be free
as their confinement
had ended.

Then
not one word
did
that
brave band
mutter,
as
they sailed
away
with
the Governor's
cutter.
Away
from
Port Jackson
away
from Australia
away from
hunger, poverty
and failure.

And at bedtime
did Mary
tell
great stories
of sailing
as
the boat
pitched
and rocked
and

the high
winds
were wailing.

Then
as darkness
fell
and the
littles ones
did sleep,
did
she sit
and stare
at the ocean
deep?
did she
resolve
that their
voyage
was going
to succeed,
for wasn't
she born
into granite
of strong
Cornish seed?

And
on those
calm nights
aboard the boat,
they must
have stared
at the stars
and thought,
and maybe

dreamt
of their
beloved England,
and how
their lives
hadn't turned
out
just as they planned.

Yet
they hung
on to
those dreams
and plans
and notions
to conquer
and sail
across
3254 miles
of ocean
That
determination
must
have been
of strong
intensity,
as
1200
of those
miles
was across
uncharted
sea.

Imagine
their feelings
when they
eventually
saw land,
on June 5th
seventeen ninety-one,
imagine
the elation,
and how
they felt
being
69 days
away
from
Port Jackson.

They had
arrived
in Kupang
and
the Island
of Timor,
where
they befriended
the Dutch
Colony
and
the friendly
Governor.
In Kupang
they
were treated kindly
and the Governor
believed
their story
that they
were survivors

from
a British ship wreck
on a night
so dark and stormy.

But one
reckless night
when William
was drinking,
he let
the true
story slip,
when
he wasn't
thinking.
He told
of how
they were
escaped
convicts
from
Botany Bay,
and how
they had
outwitted
the Governor
to get away.
He told
of how
he had
stolen
the cutter,
and tricked
the authorities,
and with
wife, children
and crew,

had
taken
to the
high seas.

Then suddenly
they were
arrested,
and yet again
chained
on a ship,
and Mary
just
could not
believe
he had
let the story
slip.
All
their dreams
were now
drowned,
and their
plans
were
just
a wreck,
and they
sat in chains
and darkness,
knee
deep in water
under the deck.

And yet again
a harrowing
predicament

had arisen,
as they
began their
way
back to England
to be caged
in Newgate
Prison.

And for
Mary
there was
yet more
tragedy
to come,
for on
that journey
she lost
her husband
daughter
and son.
From
malnutrition
and neglect,
they all died,
were
sewn
into
hessian bags,
and
slipped
over
the side.

All this
pain

and deprivation,
Mary
had to endure,
and
many months
of cruel
hardships,
before
she reached
her
English shore.

And on
their return
to Newgate
Prison,
their fate
was
to be sealed,
until
a humanitarian
called
James Boswell,
for Mary
and the crew
appealed.

This man
James Boswell
read
of the
escapees
plight,
and
could not
believe

how the crew
could have
survived
their flight.
For many
were merely
victims
of the times,
and in order
to eat
they had
committed
those crimes,
for the
country's money
on wars
had been spent,
and to ease
the country's burden
to Botany Bay or war
they were sent.

The Judge
called
them ignorant,
low life,
villains
vagabonds
and liars,
but now
James
said
they were
professional
fisher people
who had
steered
their boat
by the stars.
James said
they had
fought, and struggled
and
loved
and
lived
amid a myriad of
emotions,
had travelled
hundreds of miles
and steered their ship,
across uncharted oceans,
had suffered more
than the average
human spirit
endures,
So in fact
M 'Lord
the ignorance is
ours.

James
concluded
that
fate
had thrown
them into
adverse
circumstances,
and they

had "run their gauntlet" and taken their chances, he said they were clever Cornish fisher folk, who could not be outwitted, and the judge and the jury had to agree, and the prisoners were acquitted.

*Note number 9

12. Madron Workhouse

Misty May morning
to the workhouse, I,
silver grey green blades
soft cobwebbed
spring grasses,
tall and high.

Buttercups and daisies
on the wet wet grass
each one
a suffering spirit
of poor souls
long gone past.

The mists of a century
now fall on the land,
and barely able
to see my own hand,
I move to the wall
and take a stand

Surrounding the workhouse
the 10 foot high
heavy grey stone wall
through which walked
the sad and the grieving
the one and the all.

What lives were unravelled
what stories were told,
of the lost, the infirm
the young and the old.

What damage done
what cruelty lies
buried and hidden
under times
rolling tides.

Money for wars
money to kill
no money
for the old
the young
and the ill.

Let's march
to the tune
let's march
to the drum
to forget
those unfortunate
suffering at home.

Now the old building
lies in decay
losing more dignity
day by day.

A tile here
a brick there
slowing falling into bad
repair.

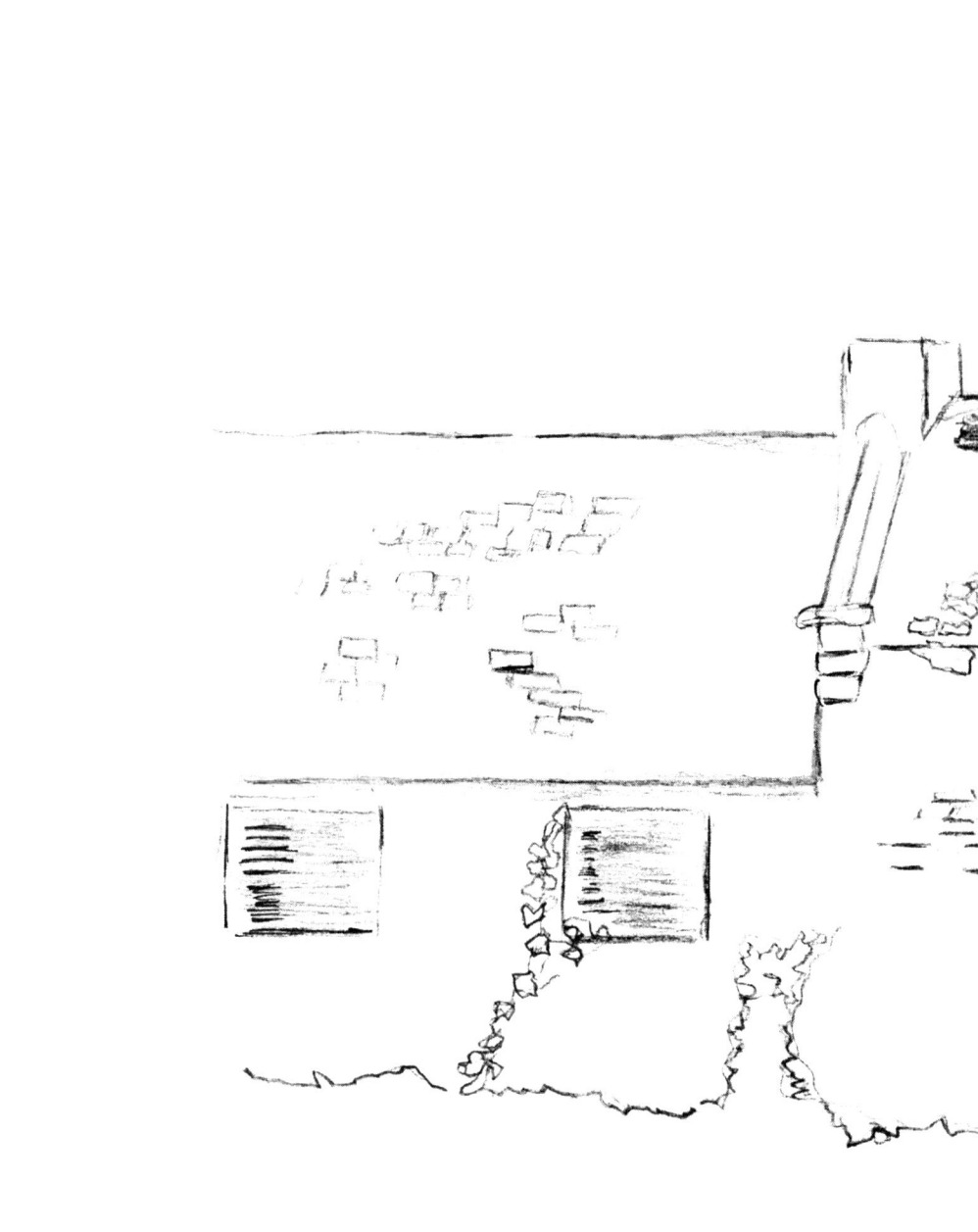

*This specimen of fine 18th Century culture
should be carefully preserved
not left to become a ruin
with never a spoken word.*

*And so slowly this house
that should be a warning to us,
will be left to crumble,
and be turned
to grey dust.*

*Note number 10

The Decaying Workhouse

13. Goodnight My Darling Bessie

When we return
to our cottage by the sea
how good
our lucky lives will be
you shall have
fine dresses of silk
fine puddings to eat
and sweets and milk

When we return
to our cottage by the sea
you shall have
fine clothes and hats
no more gruel
or cold
or rats

Now sleep
my darling Bessie
the night grows
cold and damp
the evening star
is twinkling
and the beadle
brings his lamp

And all the stars
in heaven
shine brightly
just for you
the moon
has shown
his friendly face
and sends
his love down too.

*Note number 11

14. Ding Dong Mine I

Ding Dong Mine
says 'hello'
as through
the secret
paths
we go
where
cavemen
trod
we twist
and turn
where
fires crackle
and
bracken
burn.

Generation
after
generation
since
time
began
spirit
of woman
spirit
of man
bound
in
the granite
yet
oft times
released

when
the cold
sinewy
wind
blows up
from
the
East.

The
old bell
tolls
the miners
to their
work
and
from bed
and hearth
they
rise
and
walk.

Then to
descend
down
the mine
with
candles
and canaries,
with
tales of
knockers

piskies
and fairies.

Tales
that have
survived
from the
misty past
a
phantom
that passes
with
an icy
blast.

Spirits
catching
miners
unaware,
a
tap
on the
back
a
tug
of the
hair.

Burdens
bare
heavy
each
dungeon

day,
yet
voices
from
the soul
wait
to soar
away.

Not
trapped
by timbers
dark walls
or beams
but
flying
with
Cornish
voices
on freedom's
dreams.

On the
surface
the Bal Maidens
worked
separated sorted
the tin
for a
living,
breaking
separating
griddling
and sieving.

And
what a
picture
they must
have made
as they
walked
to the mine
in white
cotton
and braid.

Their
crisp white
gooks*
like the
sails
of a
vessel
as they
crossed
the fields
past
the sheep
and the
cattle.

When
they reached
the mine
they would
change
into
hessian

And
that was
the sign
for their
work
to
begin.

Sorting
the rubble,
picking
the ore,
working
above
the shafts
on the
dressing
floor,
where
the cold
winds
blew,
and the
damp
sea mists
came in,
and
there
the Bal
Maidens
hammered
their
frames
of tin.

*wide brimmed
bonnets

And
the Cornish
workers
were religious
and proud,
and on
Sundays
attended
chapels
their voices
strong
and loud.
The fishermen
the miners
farm labourers
Bal Maidens
too,
the old and
the young
their
faith
strong and
true.

*Note number 12

15. Ding Dong Mine II

No one
knows
the
exact
date
that
Ding Dong mine
was started,
but we
do know
that
Phoenicians
and Romans
came to Cornwall
in years B.C.,
and for our tin
they
bartered.

Lots of
seafarers
and explorers
came for tin
and copper
here,
and
it's
believed
that Jesus
himself
once came
with
Joseph
of Arimathea.

Those
caravans
of merchants
came
from exotic
lands,
came
to exchange
goods
with
Cornish hands,
in exquisitely
made
vessels
from
cities
afar,
Phoenicia
Persia
Jerusalem
and Ninevah.

And so
they came
to barter
at
our humble
tin mines,
with spices
silks
cedarwood
and wines,
across
sea and moor

they forged
their trail
came for
our tin
our copper
and shale.
With them
they bought
silks
of ethereal
hue
of silver
and gold
purple,
crimson
and blue.
They came
with stories
of scrolls
and sacred bibles,
of Princes
and Kings
and
loyal
disciples.

Then
came the
Romans
with their
arrogant
demeanour,
they needed
the tin
and the

copper
for their
swords
and their
armour,
and what
a chilling
site
in a glistening
straight
line,
marching
from
Mousehole
to
Ding Dong
mine.

And
for almost
four hundred
years
they occupied
our land,
and fought
vicious
battles,
often hand
to hand
then when
Rome became
under siege
the Emperor
ordered that
they had

to leave.
They surmised
that
the British
were heathens
and a barbaric
nation,
and they
returned
to Rome
and
civilization.

And so
their
reign
ended,
and those
centuries
had passed,
and the
Romans
returned
to their
beds
and their
baths.

And
the Cornish
struggled
on,
the miners
still
deprived

of fresh
air
and
sun
and
the
basic
needs
to stay alive.
Exploited
for their
strength
and their
desperate
need, their
families
to clothe
to shelter
to feed.

Prices of
tin and
copper dropped
and wages
were low,
but then
in came
the final
blow
tin and copper
to be
imported,
shipped
across
the seas,

from
Malaysia
Indonesia
and
the East
Indies,
destroying
livelihoods
destroying
communities.

And
the mines
closed
and
were
filled
with
cement,
and
the
spirits
of the
miners
were
ours
to
lament.

Yet
sing on
for
the miners,
now
all their

work is
done,
and let
our voices
ring out
in the granite
and the stone.

And
sometimes
you
may hear
the ghosts
of the
miners
singing
heavenly
praises,
and
sometimes
you may
even
see them
through
evenings
golden
hazes.

And sometimes
you may
see a
miner's
face and
hands,
as he

travels
in the
dream
land of
gossamer
strands.

And
who knows
the
Bal Maidens
might
also be
betwixt,
the
curtain
of illusion
that hangs
'tween
this world
and the
next.

And
there
will be
a-singing
of the
hymns
and a-pouring
of the
ale
and
we can
smile

to see
the happy
ending
to this tale.

So
rise
above spirits,
rise and
and
stay,
forever
in your
golden
globe
forever
and a
day.

Rise
above
with seagull,
rise
above
with chough,
release
the power
of the Cornish,
release
the power
of love.

And
now
that

*their last
shift
is forever done,
may
the miners
sit
forever
in the
warm
Cornish
sun.*

16. The Ballad of the True Story of Eliza Jane

        ELIZA JANE:

        "Now hear me
        Bal Maidens
        when your work
        is not done,
        don't think
        you can mix
        your work
        with your fun,

        And this tale
        I tell 'ee
        to my own cost
        for not only
        my leg
        but my
        whole life
        I lost.

        I can still
        hear my mother
        on that fateful day
        I can still
        see her smile
        and the words
        she did say."

CHORUS

        MOTHER:
        "Eliza Jane Eliza Jane
        you're gonna be late
        for work again

here's your shawl
and here's your croust*
now be gone
from my hearth
be gone
from my house"

ELIZA:
How much
I did love
those sweet
summer morns
and the
precious birds
with their
chorus at
dawn,
and all
the wild flowers
were blooming
for me
on that
fateful day
in 1873.

CHORUS

MOTHER:
"Eliza Jane Eliza Jane
you're gonna be late
for work again
here's your shawl
and here's your croust

*croust – lunch

now be gone
from my hearth
be gone
from my house"

 ELIZA:
"I never
remembered
what happened
that day,
but I saw
the miners
as they knelt
to pray,
now I'm tired
of walking
along this line,
from my
Ladydowns home
to
Ding Dong Mine"

CHORUS:

 MOTHER:
"Eliza Jane Eliza Jane
you're gonna be late
for work again
here's your shawl
and here's your croust
now be gone
from my hearth
be gone
from my house"

FINAL CHORUS:
                ANGELS:
                "Eliza Jane Eliza Jane
                no more sorrow
                no more pain
                across the moors
                no more to roam
                the angels are waiting
                to carry
                you home

                The angels
                will carry
                you home."

* Note number 13

17. The Cornish Wind

Well hullabaloo
good evening
to you
I am
your
Cornish wind

I will
tumble
and crash
at your window
I will
stumble
and bash
at your door

For I
am your
Cornish Wind
from across
field
from across
moor

I will
bring
memories
of roses,
I will
bring
memories
of pain
and I will
bring
you snow
and I will
bring
you rain.

I will sweep
and swirl
around you,
keeping your
senses
sharpened
and bright,
I will
freeze
your toes
and fingertips
should
you dare
venture
out
at night

I will
rattle
the boats
in the
harbour,
I will
shake
the giant
who snores,
I will never give in
I will never give up
I am here
I am strong
I am yours.

18. The Smugglers

If you listen
carefully
you will hear
how the gale
lifts
the latch key door
my dear
and how the wind
blows from the cliffs
and shouts
for more

And then
the wind increases
to a mighty
roar
and all the
senses cease
to hold
the body
once more.

The elements
so powerful
could end
it all
for us
and in one
swift
reappraisal
be gone
before
to dust.

The wind
blows
from
the cliffs
the latchkey
lifts
in the cottage
by the sea
the timbers
creak
the roof
leaks
yet all
is as
should be.

And in
your dreams
you startle
and jump
to be amazed
the ring
of darkness
sparkles
and in
this
sleepy haze
the sound
of horses
hooves
slashing
on the granite
cold

You hear
the smugglers
laughing
then
the
masters voice
scold.

And peeping
through
the window
you see
the lanterns
blaze
as
down
to the seashore
the smugglers
make
their way

Then
through
the darkness
in the distance
you see
the vessel
in distress
the waves
dancing
madly
in their
white
ballroom dress

And
as the
evil spider
lures the
fly
to its doom
the candle light
flickers
in your
cosy bedroom.

The ship
is dashed
to pieces
against
the cruel
rocks
in vain
the crew
is heard
to cry
while
the wind
roars
and mocks
"no-one
can save
the crew"
the smugglers
maliciously
jeer.
"Tonight
we will
have

*our fill
of jewels
and food
and beer."*

*Again
the candle
flickers
the cat
stirs
on your bed
you lie
back down
to sleep
to rest
your weary
head.*

*And
in the
morning
waking
you wonder
if
t'was
a dream
and rush
to the
casement
to see
what
can
be seen.*

*And down
below
the rocks
you see
a terrible
sight,
bodies
floating
face down
that reaffirms
the night.*

19. Trengwainton

Tiptoe down
through the trees
where royal
rhododendron
stand
at ease

See the Camellia
serene and still
across a pretty bridge
and
magnificent magnolia
blossom
amongst
the dark green
foliage.

Now to the lake
where the coaches
circle around
with
ceremonial
flair,
and the scent
of the flowers
and blossoms
carousel
on the
evening
air.

From
their carriages
step

the ladies
with their
jewels
their feathers
their
fur,
top-hatted
descend
the lords
with their
canes
and their
haute couture.

Yet
please
spare a thought
for the
scullery maids
underneath
those fading
skies,
as they peep
through
polished
bannisters
with
their
tired
and
pretty
eyes.

With
a
million
lamps
the house
is lit,
candles
blaze bright
in the
hall,
moths
and music
twirl
and flit,
sweet notes
and silk dresses
swirl,
oh! those
golden memories
of when aunty
was only
a girl.

*Note number 14

20. Cold Madron Day

Chack chack
Chack chack
the small
rooks
call,
the noise
like
a brick
hitting
a wall,
it's too
cold
for us
to sing today,
our beaks
are cold
our feathers
are clay.

Through
the gnarled
cracked bare
branches
of the old
oak tree
the cruel
wind
blows,
while the
small birds
clutch on
with their
cold bare
toes,

like statues
in
their
stiff repose.

Around
and down
the branches
swirl
and then
again
they
rise,
the tiny
birds
still cling
on,
as if hypnotised.

Again
the white
wind
gushes,
and
gives
a mighty
roar,
but
it's
merry
go round
riders
are hanging
on,

"Can we
go round
just
once
more?"

Chack chack
chack chack
above the
graveyard
towards
the carn,
see how
the giant
clouds
twist
and turn,
from
the land
to
the heavens
and back,
chack chack
chack chack.

White
on white
the colours
of the
cold,
towering
clouds
of pink
ribbons
of
gold,
ice blue

thoughts
vibrate
on a
grey
gravel
track
chack chack
chack chack.

A wintry
sun
slides
behind
the cemetery
wall
bidding
a cold
farewell
to
us all,
and then
setting
on
both
good and ill,
rolls
behind
the ancestral
hill,
and
as we
can never
turn
our clock
back,
chack chack
chack chack.

The Fantasy Years

21. *Ebb and Flow*

Across
the land
we lived in
we dreamt
our lives
away
and seeing
love
with
all its
power
we knew
we must
obey
the laws
of nature
that
bind us
the coils
of love
that
entwine
us
the sea
of love
that
surrounds
us
then ebbs
and flows
away.

Yet
at night
the piskies
and
the fairies
kept
vigil
at
our cottage
door,
weaving
their
lanterns
to and fro
across
the fields
up from
the shore.

22. The Gypsy Girl of Morvah - Part 1

I wish I had a room
the gypsy girl said
with a cat
and some flowers
and somewhere
to lay my head.

And if I had
that room
the gypsy girl said,
I could sit
in my armchair
or dream
on my bed.

Her beauty
was unearthly
her dark tresses
curled
and when
her orbital
eyes opened
her long lashes
unfurled.

Her ruby red lips
held all
under her spell
first she would
kiss
then fine stories
she would tell.

Yet the
raggle taggle gypsies
just laughed
at her dreams,
but laughter
turned to horror
when,
lying
by the campfire
they heard
unearthly
screams.

In the majestic
manor house
the Lord and Lady
lived
but he had
taken
gypsy girl
as his
mistress
and his
wife
could not
forgive.

And in
her rage,
his wife
had
killed
him,
in their
elegant
bedroom,
he fell
from the
veranda
where
the
honeysuckle
bloom.

She ripped
the curtains
down
from the old
four poster
bed
she slashed
through
the pillows
where
his mistress
had laid
her head

She slashed
the velvet
curtains
and the
tapestries

On the wall
she slashed
the silken
ottoman
and her black
lace
Spanish
shawl.

Heartbroken
and alone
down
the wall
she did
slip
and slide
while
the wind
and gales
and rain
whirled
and wailed
outside

Around
the campfire
not a
word
was spoken
all
eyes gazed
at the
sobbing
girl
whose dreams
had just

been
broken.

He promised
me everything
the gypsy
girl said,
he promised
me
the world
and
now
he is dead.
And
all I
ever wanted,
the gypsy
girl said,
was a
room
with a
cat and
some
flowers
and
somewhere
to lay
my head.

I will
never
have the
cat
or room
and my
true love
is dead,
and I
will take
wild flowers
today
to lay
above
his
head.

23. The Gypsy Girl of Morvah - Part II

She took the path
down to the cliffs,
for answers she did search
then decided on
what she would do
as she passed
the humble church.

Yet love
was all around her
from the warm granite
from the warm ground
but in her fog of sorrow
she couldn't see
the beauty
all around.

She couldn't smell
the pure sweet herbs
the chives or thee yarrow,
she couldn't hear
the singing birds
the robin
or the sparrow.

The foxgloves cried
"Go back, go back"
the campion
they cried too,
the buttercups
shed tears in vain
but she knew
what she must do.

The bluebells blessed her
with all their strength
whilst daisies and dandelions
tugged at her feet,
from golden bushes
white butterflies flew
to whisper softly
"retreat, retreat".

Bright
as heaven
shone
the golden yellow gorse
but
even this
could not
ease her pain
nor change
her chosen
course.

And then the sea
came into view
the cliffs
the universe
to live
a life
of shame
and hate
or die
which
could be
worse?

Then down past
the Holy Well
and down into
the deep sea swell
past azure lights
and glittering pools
and open caskets
of priceless jewels,
yet none
could her pretty frame
surpass,
not the pearl necklace
not the diamond clasp.

And regal Neptune
did come to respect
and laid her across his arms,
and the old church bells
did chime under the sea,
against
a world full of
hatred and harms.

And this
was the last sound
the gypsy girl heard
and Neptune
the last creature to see,
and now
although the deed
has been done
at last she is finally free.

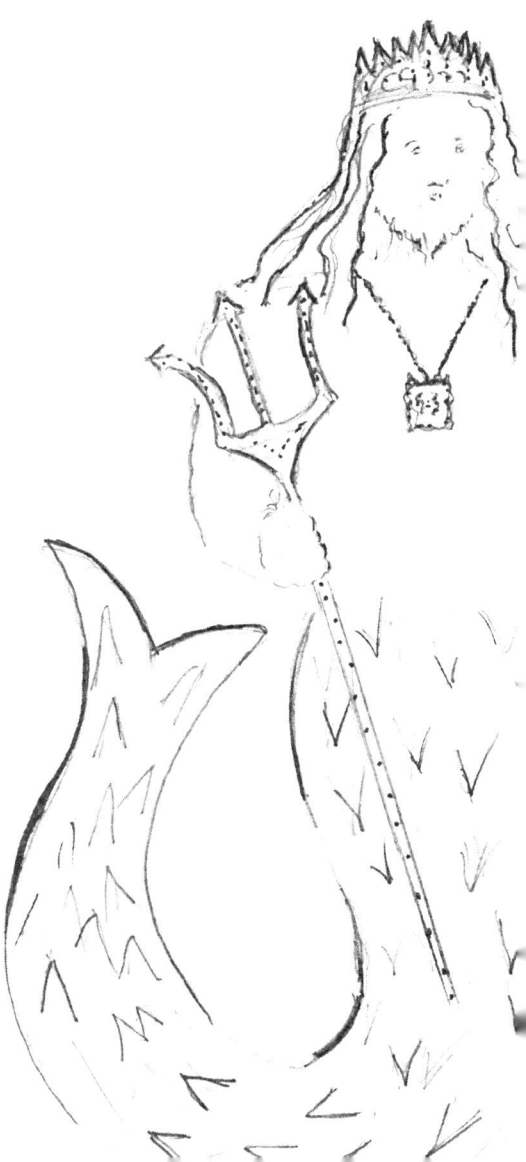

24. The Ghost of the Gypsy Girl Morvah - Part III

The Ghost
girl
she moved
and white
was she,
as white
as the foam
on the raging
sea.

The Ghost girl
she moved
and black
was she,
and black
the abyss
where
her eyes
should
be.

The Ghost
girl
she moved
and Kitty
understood,
for she saw
her pain
neath her cloak
neath
her
hood.

*Kitty is the protagonist in my next novel

25. The Mermaid of Morvah

And in the darkness
she did sit
deep in deepest thought
and on that rock
she pondered
where lay
the comfort
that
she sought.

The planet
spun around her
beneath her
and above,
the moon did
light the night
and the sea
did speak
with love.

Go to your children
they need you
so much now
hold them,
wrap them in your heart
do not
let them go.

And the waves
did crash
and weave
and wallow
then rush

and laugh
and play
and twinkling
moonbeams
caressed
the water
as on
the rock
she lay.

Into the velvet
stream of water
she did slip and slide
and as the moon
laughed down
onto the sparkly
planet
beneath
the seaweed
she did
glide.

And if
on magic moonlit
nights
you sit beside the sea
and glimpse
a shimmering form
beneath the waves,
you know who it will be.

26. Mischievous Piskies

Folks
d'ask
"are
em real?"
and
while
they
ponder
us'll
steal,
into
yer
cottage
into
yer
'omestead,
there
to meck
mischief
in
chair
couch
'n bed.
an'
while
ee
stand
a'skritchin
of yer
'ead
us'll
be
gone
gigglin'
with
yer
milk
an'
yer
bread.

*See note no. 4

27. An April Awakening

"Would man but wake from out his haunted sleep, Earth might be fair and all men glad and wise."

CLIFFORD BAX, 1886.

The waves
are really
choppy
on the sea
today
the seagulls
laugh
and swirl
and the
mermaids
play.

The wind
whispers
wildly
across the
fields
today
the yellow
gorse
shines
bright
and the
daffodils
sway.

The ancient
Stone age
dwellings
stand still
and firm
and strong
as the ghosts
of our
forefathers
sing
the warrior
song.

Then
suddenly
the
whole sky
lights
up
in a
golden
yellow
hue,
and
down
to the

sea
the light is
streaming on
fish
and
mermen
dreaming
too.

Illuminated
on the
soft
granite
wall
the velvet
foxgloves
stand
alert
and
tall,
and
as
sentinel
as
gentle
gentlemen.

Then
a golden
capsule
appears
through
the
light
and
lands
upon
the
ground,
and
blows
the
waves
into
high
walls
of
foam
and
surf
which
cascades
all
around.

Then
a low
voice
from
beyond
the
machine
calls

"Quickly
come
with us"
and
queues
of
speechless,
staring,
people
and
animals
line up
to
ride
on the
golden
'air bus'.

Then
time
passes
and the
capsule
closes,
leaves
behind
the
foxgloves
and
roses,
leaves
the
bee
who
on
the

buttercup
dozes,
leaves
slumbering
souls
in soft
reposes.

And
already
this
capsule
is
one million
light
years
away
while
the
granite
stays
the same
as
yesterday,
smiling,
warm,
and
forever
grey.

And
now
this
golden
ark
of

goodly souls, is travelling across the universe to achieve their goals, and has gone to build a new life, in their City of Gold.

28. The White Owl Angel: For Marjorie & Cathy

In
her cape
of billowing
white,
through
the soft
navy blue
of night,
the snowy
owl
appeared.

Like
a phantom
in the
sky,
through
times
of bleak
uncertainty,
the snowy
owl
steered.

Cut glass
crystal
stars
dropped
their lights
like
crystal
tears
and her
ritual
was
begun.

Circling
circling
like
an origami
bird
and
not a
sound
was heard
as around
me she
spun.

And as
we flew
through
the air
together
not a sound
not a sound
as we
flew
through
the air
together
around
and around.

And she
whispered
as I
fell,
so deep
under
her spell,
"This is
your heaven
don't
make it
your hell."

And
the message
that the
white
owl brought
was to
remind us
that our
lives are
short,
and all
our troubles
will amount
to nought,
and to pray
and be
silent
in silent
thought.

1800's - 1900's

Alfred Wallis was born in Devonport in August 18th 1855. He moved to Cornwall and didn't start painting until he was 70 years old. Alfred painted with children's paints on any materials which came to hand. (See 'Dandelions and Snails').

29. My poem for Alfred Wallis, Painter 1855-1942.
The Improvisers

And did the soft caterpillar realise
he would always have to improvise
when could he be 'Knight' and rise
to join the other 'butterflies'.

We children and Alfred
experienced the same
a go-cart buggy
from an old pram frame
a precious dolly
from a log of wood
a gifted painter
misunderstood.

A sketch of the sea
on a cardboard box
one eye on the mast
one eye on the docks.

My baby sister sleeps
in my dolly's pram
mothers at the round table
making tarts of jam.

A Dick Turpin mask
from a black velvet frock
a sketch of a fish
on a granite rock.

Now Alfred's hair
is long and white
his beard
is turning grey,
he'll soon return
to his childhood home
he'll see them all
one day.

The wind blows through
the hawthorn bushes
rhododendrons bloom bright
on the carn
Alfred sleeps
in his
wrought iron bed
his sea
a peaceful calm.

*Note number 15
*Alfred died in Madron Workhouse in August 1942.

30. *My poem for Sven Berlin – Painter, Sculpture, poet, author, 1911-1999*

Fragments

Fragmentations of reality
chip chip
the fragments fly
desperate
to see the whole picture
but this world is just a lie.

In his coat of many colours
chip chip
the fragments fly
misunderstood and starving
for this world
is just a lie.

Chisel, pen, pencil or brush
chip chip
the fragments fly
choose your weapons wisely
for this world
is just a lie.

In egocentric circles
the accusations fly
hypocrisies
confusion
for this world
is just a lie.

31. *My Poem for Sydney Graham, Born in Scotland, moved to Cornwall 1918 – 1986.*

Captain

The Captain of the written word
raised his compound head
and reading from lines
he had just penned
softly and slowly
he read.

And there we sat together
in the gathering gloom
while Sydney's words
tumbled
into the rustic granite room

Had we but known
what lay in store
could we
have steered
our ship to shore?

1930's
The Approach of World War

32. Which way is the wind blowing?

Which way is the wind blowing
who knows, who knows
to which war are the young men going
who knows, who knows
the winds of war
blow fierce and strong
and carry both evil and good along.

Tyrants
plot wars
in their
brand new suits
for money
and for fame
while young men
die
in their brand new boots
only
just pawns
in the game.

The Battle of Britain: 1940 – 10th July – 31st October

33. Cheer Up Old Boy

When the call
came to scramble,
to scramble to the sky,
my heart missed a beat
and I thought
that I would die.

Then a reassuring hand
upon my back,
a soft whisper
through the rain,
"Cheer Up Old Boy
we'll soon be home again."

Jack Pengelly was
a Methodist man
and his faith
it was strong,
and with his words
inside my head
I pushed myself along.

Then came the fight
each man alone,
and even
in the heat
of battle,
cold blooded
to
the bone.

Like
goldfish panicking
in a bowl,
rolling
all around,
sometimes sideways
sometimes forward
sometimes upside down.

Into
the tumbling insanity
of the crude
roulette game,
not to prosper
but to kill
destroy
and maime.

Returning to the mess
I saw the empty chair
where Pengelly would sit
and take
the cool night air,
a sharp arrow
hit my heart
and a voice came through
quite plain
"Cheer Up Old Boy
We'll soon be home again."

Now years have gone
and I sit in peace
and read
my silent tome,
and my mind will drift
and I'll remember
the boys
who didn't make it home.

Then always in my inner ear
like a spirit from his plane
I feel his hand upon my back
and his soft whisper
in the rain
"Cheer Up Old Boy
We'll soon be home again."

*Note number 16

<u>1944 – 6th June D Day</u>

34. 'D' Day – 'The Place of No Sorrow'

And the sea held those precious bodies
those fathers, those lovers, those sons
their eyes holding tears of salt water
while they danced to the tune of the guns
they tumbled and rolled with the pebbles
those brothers, those uncles, those braves
some wearily crashing onto the beach
some clamped in watery graves
return to your homelands and loved ones
please don't die on this godforsaken beach
return to that place of no sorrow
where your sweetheart's arms
are within reach.

1945
Post War Cornwall

35. Stillness

Stillness
in
the heart
of time
crushed
the flowers
that
were thine

Now
The petals
fall
and they
scatter
down
those streams
that
gush
and splatter
and
the only
things
that
mattered
are our
dreams
laid bare
in painful
tatters.

Tears
of forgetfulness
add
to
the stream
they
float
on past
transparent
unseen.

Oh
glassy
water
cold
reflecting
can
we float
down
unsuspecting
will
we
ever again
dance
and sing
or will
we always
be
remembering?

Flow
down
my
heart

to
yesterday
where
love
was true
and
children
play and each
day
brought
the
rainbows
end
where
we
our
humble
lives
could
mend.

36. The Healing Has Begun

The seasons slip past
green turns to brown
to rust
to grey
our lives
float past
in
peaceful
disarray.

And we begin
to mend our lives
to put together
the broken pieces
to heal
those wounds
that war
inflicts
as now
the fighting
ceases.

Yet
somewhere
in a
sunkissed
clearing
on leaves
and heather
and moss
an
angel
lies weeping,

for such
cruelty,
such
hatred,
such loss.

37. **Destiny**

In the hollow
of a silence
after
the crashing
of
the trees,
Destiny
comes calling
from her home
amid
the seas.

In
her white dress
she comes
calling,
from her hands
the foxgloves
falling
while all
around
the granite
whispers
in
the breeze.

You can hide
yet
she will
find you
with her
velvet gown
she will
bind you
put your
shattered
past
behind you
and bow
to Destiny.

With
the stars
and moon
to guide you
and Destiny
beside you
your strength
will always
find you
sweet sister
Destiny.

38. Carbon to Carbon

I hear their yodelling*, here they come
their axes glistening in the cold sun
back to bond with the trees and the crows
to find their roots I suppose
and if you cut me down today
will I cry or try
to run away.

If a howling wind should blow me down
then to the elements
I must yield
my body lying slain
sixty foot
across the farmer's field
my being ripped
reluctantly
from the
sodden ground
my roots exposed
redundantly
cruelly
placenta round.

So chop me up
to burn on your fires
at least I can leaves drop
on your dreams and desires
I can whirl and spark
like a manic banshee
and crackle and spit
whilst making your tea.

And then I will forgive you
whilst I listen

to your woody jargon
for beneath our very souls
are we not all
just carbon to carbon?

* Note number 17
*The Woodcutters loved to yodel, axes thrown over their shoulders, on their way to chop down trees.
* The Woodcutters first banded together in a cottage called Cae-Einion in North Wales in 1945. They then moved to Lamorna in 1947.

39. Lamorna: The Woodcutters

When
the Woodcutters
first came
to Lamorna
they came
on foot,
tired
and weary
from
war time,
some
had fought
and
some
had not.

Whether
soldier
or
conscientious
objector,
they all
had crosses
to bare
all with
years of
conflict
and oppression
and all
had stories
to share.

All had
years of
deprivation
and
dodging
bombs
and so
on the
wild rugged
cliffs
at Lamorna
they decided
to set up
their
homes.

And there
with
their simple
possessions:
tent, knife
spoon and axe
they at
last
could lay
aside
for a while,
their
dusty
brown boots
and rucksacks.

And soon
with
their wives
and their
children
they dreamed
of a brave
new world,
as they
stretched
on the
rocks
in the sunshine
and their
layers of
anguish
unfurled.

The locals
called them
'Billy Goats'
as
with
long beards
and
bronzed torsos
around the cliffs
they
scampered,
no more
by
wartime troubles
hampered.

Their axes
were long
and sharp
each
6 to 9 inches
long,
for they cut down
their timber
to buy
their food,
and with
positivity
they were
strong.

Originally
the
Woodcutters
had met
in North Wales
whilst
working
for the
Forestry Commission,
and in
a tumble down
cottage
in Dolgellau
they
created
their new
future
vision.

They were a band of conscientious objectors, philosophers and radical thinkers, they planned to re-educate the world to heal and to remove the blinkers.

They would read, philosophise, and debate and used wisely the post-war space, they had a whole new world to create if they were to save

the human race. And they felt they should let bygones be bygones as they headed for their new horizons.

At Lamorna the sun shines on the sea and I recall those long gone years, how the planet has not learnt it's lesson yet for we

still
have
those
mortal fears.

Now
we can
only
look back
with
rose tinted
eyes,
dreaming
about those
past days,
under
sanguine
Lamorna
skies. *

* Note number 17

To read more about the Woodcutters, "Dandelions and Snails" by
A.C. Miles-Smith

1950's
The Austerity Years

For Ann Newport

40. The Tumbling Year

<u>Spring</u>

Slowly
we awake
from hibernation
to begin
our yearly
deliberation.
The blossoms
start
to fill
the land
and
wishing well
fairies
dance
hand in hand.

April brings
the spring
rains
and it's
off
to school
with
growing
pains.
Up to Ding Dong
to catch
the bus,
old coats

on heads
to shelter
us.

At Ding Dong
we see
the wild
sea foam
and hide
the old
coats
under
bushes
for our
return
walk
home.

In Madron
school rooms,
the coal fires
are lit,
and clothes
are draped
on fire guards
to dry
in front
of it.

In the wild wind
outside

the schoolroom,
the
gravestones
stiffen,
and through
the window
you hear
"Listen, listen
It won't be long,
It won't be long"
as the children
sing
their favourite
song
deep from the
heart
and gustily
"For those in
Peril
on the sea."

May Day
brings
kisses
and pledges
while
sweethearts
meet
in haystacks
and
hedges.

Summer

Dawn breaks
and baby cries
the children rub
their tired eyes
mother sits
drinking tea
then rallies
her children
1, 2, 3.
C'on m'dears
here we go
all for the sake
of the humble
potato.

Now hands
with dirt
soon are
coated,
and soil
gets under
nails.
Children
struggle
with
heavy loads
and handles
clank on
wrought iron
pails.

Then
the old
farmer's
boots
crunch
on dusty
lane,
and from
his
tattered
waistcoat
hangs
a golden
watch chain.

Then the
farmer
rakes the earth
behind the
children
with
a stick
shouting
"Scrabble
for em
kids
be quick
be quick
fast
as you can
now
a shilling
a bag
fast
as you can,
don't lag
don't lag."

The day
is dry,
the sun
is hot
each child's
face of
soil
and snot,
the day
passes
slowly
like
the land
time
forgot.

Then
from
behind
the hedge
pipe smoke
rises,
at last
the signal
that
the day
demises,
the workers
wend homeward
while
the evening
creeps,
slowly
to bed
with
the cows
and
the sheep.

Autumn

Now
is
the harvest home
the sheaves
of wheat
the bales
of corn,
the
Van Gogh
birds
fly low
and full,
feasting
on
the fare
as well.

In
the little
chaple
the singing
rings
embracing
childish
imaginings,
and
with
happy
hearts
we
sing
of ploughing
the earth
and scattering,
while
in
polished
pews,
the
giggling
and
the
chattering.

Then
russet red,
the
leaves
will
fall,
while
memories
of summer
start
to pall,
and
all the
children
now are
scratched
and
scrumbled
as
in the
bramble
hedges
they've
tracked
and
tumbled
for
mother
to
make
the
blackberry
crumble.

Winter

Bonfires
burn
and air
is smoke
filled,
noses
are red
and
fingers
are
so
chilled.
East
winds
begin to
blow
cold,
across
field
barn, moor
and fold.
Children
collect firewood
from
the carn,
circling their
arms
to try
to keep warm.

Then
snow
descends
and
silences
the crew
fingers
are purple
and
lips
are blue.

Giant
skies
are bare
and
starry,
the
children
speed home
and
do not
tarry.

Then
the fire
is lit,
and
the
old black
kettle
is
full,
and
the
burnt,
smoked
tea
tastes
wonderful.

Dedicated to Ann Newport nee Strick, daughter of Hilda Strick, who was a good friend of my mother, Marjorie, and of our family.

41. Sweetness – From Beyond Morvah Church

Sweetness
came to me
across the fields
up from the sea,
it spoke of
childhood days
and blossoms
on the tree.

When Jesus
was a little boy
he too played
in the fields
he broke a branch
from the hawthorn tree
he ripped
his gown
on thorns
he should have stayed
he would have been
safe
in Cornish arms.

Sweetness
came to me today
it spoke
of childhood days
it kissed
the cobwebs
in the barn
and spoke
in whispering
phrase.

It spoke
of childhood days
with voices
from the past
it flew around
the old churchyard it shook
the swaying mast
with a skip
and a hop
it then was gone
to where
I never asked.

42. That Hot June Day

Deep
lay
the
foreboding
furrows
dark
brown
and
long.

Green
and
healthy
the
thick
potato
plants
standing
strong.

Hot
the sun
on
the baked
earth
so
dried.

Wet
those
tears
on our
hands
as we
cried.

That
hot
day
mother
gave
birth
under
the
leaking
eave.

Where
the
industrious
spider
did web
and
did
weave.

The
sun
shone
through
the broken
skylight
window
on
shafts
of fairy
dust.

And
on
those
sunbeams
we heard the
whisper
"Don't trust
Don't trust
Don't trust".

Yet
the clock
ticking
on the
bureau
declared
"You must
You must
You must".

Now
as we
stand
silently,
in the
place
of our
birth,

*our
tears
fill
the
furrows
and
return
to the
earth.*

43. Fallow But Not Forgotten

Whilst
walking
through
the fallow
fields
an object
caught
my eye,
a
triangular
piece
of blue
pottery,
a relic
of years
gone
by.

And
I pondered
on who
had drunk
from
the cup,
this
worker
in
the
field.

And
I wondered
how
many years
of history,
was
slowly
being
revealed.

And
Looking
more
closely
I then
found,
hundreds
of
pieces
of pottery,
scattered
on
the
ground.

Most
of them
were
bright
patterns
decorated
with
bright glaze
of
china blue
and
some
were
painted
with pink
flowers
from
the women
who
worked
in the
field
too.

And
to teacups
and
farm
labourers
my
thoughts
drifted
back,
and
especially
to my
mother,
who
had
to work,
in headscarf,

wellingtons
and dusty
old
mac.

And
I thought
of all
the
mothers
and the
sacrifices
they
had
made,
in order
to
feed
their children
from
the plough,
the rake
and the
spade.

Then
I knew
this
field
was not
fallow,
but
rich
were its
words
and its
seams,

and though
the years
may
roll on
and
pass
forever
always
the
same
are our
hopes
and our
dreams.

For
the
field
had given
forth
it's heaven,
and
the field
had
given
forth
it's hell,
and the
ghosts had
liberated
the
hopes and
the dreams
of the
workers,
now
ready

to
tell.

And
in
that
shivering
smokey
mist,
I felt
the
cool
night
air
and
before
me rose
the faces,
the stories
of the
workers who
had
once
toiled
there.

Then
shadows
started
to lengthen
and creep
and
dusk
started
to fall
and
from

the
charcoal
tree tops
the
crows
made
their
bedtime
call.

And again
I thought
of my mother,
my past
life
and
how
lucky
now
are we,
no longer
shivering
under
old coats
nor
collecting
firewood
to
make
our
tea.

And
slowly
I headed
homeward,
with my
bag
of precious
pot,
to make
a collage
and a
shrine
and pay homage,
to the
workers
we
all
forgot.

44. René's Bridge

I called
to see
René
and
peeped
around
her door
"Come in
if you're
good looking"
she
joked
with a
roar.
So I
stepped
inside
intrigued
to talk
more.

I asked
her
what
she had
thought
of my
book,
and
she answered
with

a mystical
look,
"It took
me
back"
said
René
"Right back
to the
days
of my
youth,
and
as I
read
your
poems
the
words
did
heal
and soothe."

For
there
in the
fields
our mother
had to
struggle
and

strive,
and
work in
all weathers
just to
keep
us alive."

"Then
my mother
became
ill
from the
rain
and the
cold,
it's
double
pneumonia
us
children
were
told."

"And
Vernon
my brother
took
over the
role
of

breadwinner
for
our family
at
14 years
old."

And René
seemed
to have
light
behind
her
face
and her
eyes,
and through
her pain
and her
anguish the
yearning
for lost
family
ties.

And
for days
I could
see her
face,
and the
light
that
behind
her had
shone,
and

when I
called again
to see
René
a bare
house told me
she had
gone.

For
that day
she had
spoken,
she had
pointed
away
to the
west,
across
to Boswarthen
where
her soul
might
find
rest.

1960's
The Swinging Sixties

45. The Sixties – For Diane and John

And
then the
sixties
came along
with
fabulous
fashions,
optimism
and song.

And there
was a
liberalizing
of
thought
and attitude
and
as in the
"Roaring Thirties"
we
were really
"In the mood".

And we
sang and
laughed
and laughed
and sang
and
like birds
uncaged
our spirits
rang,
and as

the Beatles
staged
their symphonies,
a British
generation
could
rest at
ease.

There
was
'Top of the Pops'
and
'Ready Steady Go'
and
the nation
basked
in its
psychedelic
glow.

And
trendy
boutiques
hit
the
streets
with
floral
flounces,
and
kipper
ties
and

there
were
budding
romances,
between
dolls and
guys.

And while
for our
decadent
ways
we became
fond,
things
were not
as good
across
the pond.

Whilst
Harold
Wilson
kept our
troops
out of
Vietnam,
the young
American guys
had to
fight for
Uncle Sam.

Yet
the universe
is still
learning,
and we
must strive
to end war,
For there
will be
a day
when war
is no more

Diane & John Slater on
their wedding day,
Penzance Registry Office
25th March 1971

when flower power
is eternal
and love
has found
its way,
and
Diane and John,
are
still
together
today

46. The Blacksmith and The Ballerina

The blacksmith
and the ballerina
dwelt
in the
same hamlet,
and
although
they
admired
each other
from afar,
years
past
them by
and they
had
never met.

Each day
he worked
at his
fire
dreaming
as
through
the window
the light
came
streaming.

He worked
with
precision
and
thoughts
impassioned

and
through
this medium
his
objects
were
fashioned.

Each
day
he
saw her
through
his
latticed
windows,
as
she
danced
and tripped
on her
tiny toes.

The
tapping
hammer
were
her
tapping
steps,
and
the
furnace
flames,
her
lovely

arms
outstretched,
sideways
and
upwards
they
rose
and
meandered,
up
to
the very
stars
they
wandered.

And so
his thoughts
did
twist
and
curve
and twirl,
manifesting
into
shapes
and objects
of his
ballerina
girl.

And
sometimes
she
peeped
into

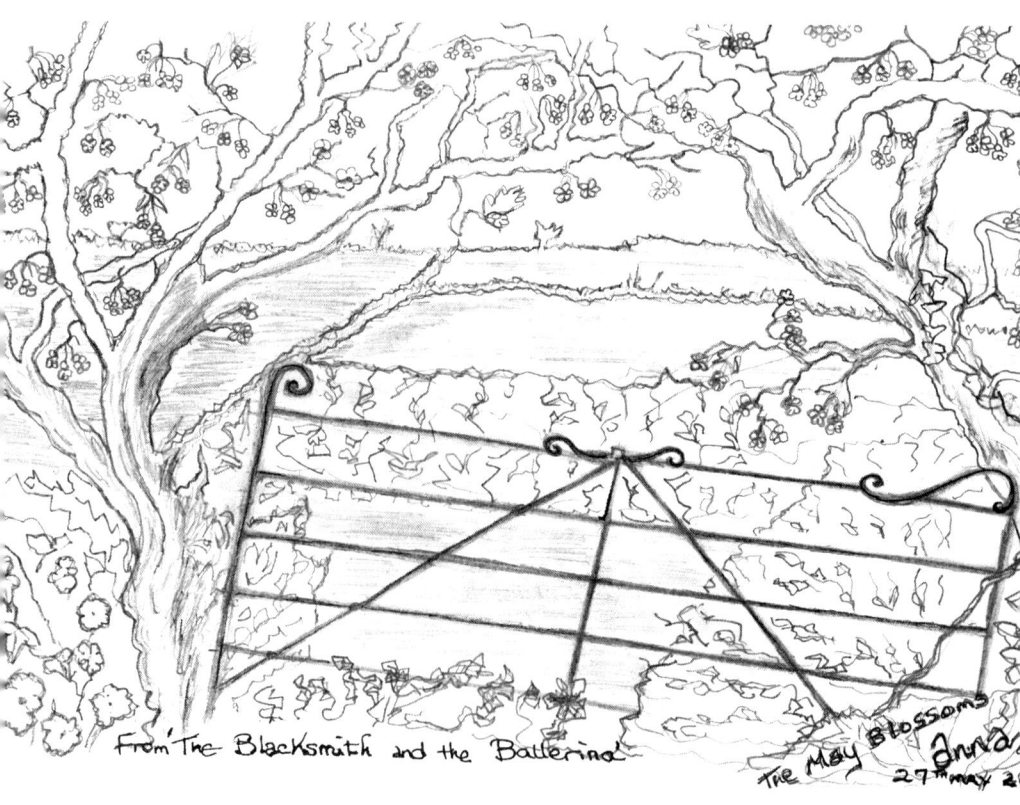

the window
to see,
his thoughts
tumbling
into
his
creativity.

Then
one day
the ballerina's
fame
took her
away
from
the hamlet
and
flame,
took her
away
to far
away
places,
new cities
new towns
new theatres
and faces.

And
she lost
herself
under
the glamour
and
praise
and
dissolved
under

the weight
of a
thousand
bouquets.

Now
time
had passed
for
the
blacksmith,
and
the gates
wheels
and
hooves
were
gone,
and
behind
the
door
on a
rusty
old
nail
hung
his
dusty
old
apron.

And
time
had
passed
for the
ballerina

as
well,
and
the day
dawned,
on her
last
farewell.

So
she
scooped
up
her
flowers
and
made
her
retreat,
through
autumns
leaves
which
fell
at her
feet.

The
pretty
pumps
she
hung
up
in her
hall,
and
her
dress

and
hair net
were
rolled
into
a
ball.

She
returned
to the
old
hamlet
to ponder
and to
rest,
and
could
not
decide
if it
had
been
for
the
best.

For
she
missed
the theatre
the stage
and
her friends,
although
she
knew

all
good
things
must come
to an end.

So
she
deemed
to
cross
the
fields
to
see,
if
once
more
she
might
live
in
her
old
country.

And
still
to
his
memory
the
blacksmith
often
strayed,
thinking
about

all
the objects
he
had
made,
and
wondering
if
in time
they
had
stayed.

So
he
deemed
to
cross
the
fields
to
see,
if
the
old
iron
gate
still
stood
in
the
lee.

And
there
was
the

old gate, a product of his analytical thought, despite now leaning on hawthorn trees for support.

And there was also a familiar figure, leaning on the gate for support, whilst gazing into the valley deep in deepest thought.

The ballerina turned to him and gave a beautiful smile, and for the first time he realised she was quite shy and fragile.

And he gave her his hand and they both knew right away, each recognising the other's vulnerability.

And there, next to the gate, under the hawthorn boughs, together at last they took their vows, with the Vicar, the trees, the crows and the cows.

Now they dance

*into
their
dream
of
the
wheel,
flower,
piano,
and
cart,
into
their
land
of
the
molten
heart.*

*And
moulded
together
in
a
forge
of
pli-és,
they
swirl
forever
into
their
forever
days.*

*To Be In Harmony
With Nature
and the Universe*

To Be In Harmony with Nature and the Universe

47. *Reynard the Fox*

In olden days
many stories
were written
about
our friend
the ancient
Briton.

Songs
were sung
of the brave
and
the bold
and around
many
firesides
history
was told.

Stories
about
how cunning
and
wise
is
Reynard
The fox
with
his
elliptical
eyes.

How
while
the farmer snores
in his
sleep,
across
the
Cornish
country
side,
the fox
will
creep.

His
top coat
is
of
red-brown
russet,
his
white
tipped tail,
the
brush
hunters
covet.

The front
of the
fox's
limbs
are black,
as are
his ears
and
his back.

In April
the baby
cubs
arrive,
and
then
the vixen
must
strive,
to guard
them
carefully,
and at
one month
old,
take
them out,
to be
brave
and bold.

She will
gather
them

together,
and
on moor
and
in heather
they will
search
for
beetles
slugs
and snails
and
whatever
other
insect
prevails.

On the
seashore
they will
search
for
crabs
in their
shells,
and
she
will
teach
them
how to
fend
for themselves.
Maybe
they will
find
cockles

and mussels
and
she will
patiently
endure
their
tumbles
and tussels.

Back
in the
fields
Vixen
stands
statuesque,
listening
for
signals
through
granite
and ground,
astutely
aware
that her
family's
survival
depends
on reaction
to sight
and to
sound.

Then
vixen
feels
a cold
shiver

on that
bracken
crackling
Christmas Eve,
and
tip toeing
from behind
the fern
and the heather
she knows
it's time
to leave.

She
smells
the winds
that
blow
through
the grasses,
she
senses
each
season
as it
passes.

Knows
that the
holly
berry
forecasts
snow,
knows
when
her family
must

stay
or go.

She
watches
the winter
sun
in its
high isolation,
as it
charts
its winter
path from nation
to
nation.

As she
follows
the suns
journey
from
east to
west
she
feels
uneasy
and
cannot
rest,
knows
this time
is not
the best.

Again
she
raises

her
noble
head,
and
one
million
years
of wisdom,
warn
her of
dread.

Then
did
we hear,
on
that icy,
cold
Christmas
morn,
the
harrowing
sound
of the
huntsman,
blowing
his horn.
"Goodwill
to all men!,
but
damn
the fox,
cut off
his head,
put it
in a box."

A
flash
of a
red coat,
the strike
of horses
hooves,
Reynard
picks up
his ears
and like
lightening he
moves.
His red
red heart
beats
like a drum,
as over
the hillside
the death
men
come.

30 to one,
the dogs
jump on,
see
the body
squirm
and
flail,
attack
his body
and
cut off
his
tail.

And in
this
mix of
blood
and faeces,
they rip
old Reynard
to bits
and
pieces.

Then
to the
pub
to sing
and drink
port
"Cheers
Merry Christmas!
Oh what
a
sport"!

* Note number 18

Foxes have existed in Britain for over 1 million years.

48. Brock the Badger

Moonlit night
still
the glade
long dark
shadows
that the
thick trees
made
as
they stand
as elephants
of stone
and jade
and
wait for
Brock
to be
betrayed.
Statues
under
a glass
dome
in a
marbleized
environment
of
their
very own.

Yet
hark
a snuffle
and a
scuffle,
here
Brock
comes,
can
he hear
the jungle
drums?,
as through
the
molten leaves
he will
shuffle,
with his
twitching
snout,
then
a sniff
and another
snuffle,
is there
danger
about?

Here
comes
Brock
to the
tune
of the
fairy
pipes,
in his
camouflage
suit
of
black
and white
stripes,
and
through
the
bracken
and the
moist
foliage,
Brock
the
badger
takes
his
stage.

He
lives
outside
the human
form
awake
from
sundown
until
the dawn,
and
although
he is
of
roguish
renown,
his
name
has been
given
to many
a town:

Brockham
Brockholes
and
Brockenhurst,
these
are the
towns
he
frequented
first.

On his
fur
he spreads
seeds
from hedge
to hedge,
the wild
flowers
of our
English
Heritage,
with primrose,
campion,
foxglove,
wild rose
and
bluebell,
he
showers
our
carpets
from
dell to
dell.

In forests
of old
our
ancient
fren*
had
to fear
the
hunting
men,
but
in
winter
when
the land
was
covered
in
snow,
underground
with
his
clan
old
Brock
could go.

Badger's
skin
is loose
upon
his back,
if wolf
or bear
tried

to attack,
he
had
the chance
to turn
and
fight
back.

Yet now
the badger
is tricked
and hated
his
opposition
cold
and calculated,
his
foe
no longer
roars
in rage,
his foe
is now
the silent
cage.

He doesn't
deserve
to be
victimized
he doesn't
deserve
to be
so despised.

* FREN = Friend and enemy

Science
can help
but no
one
will
pay,
they would
rather
see
old Brock
fade
away.
And who
are we
to condemn
and preach?
he leaves
no plastic
on the
beach.

And now
a
black
and white
flash
through
the trees,
or
is it
just
moonbeams
that
one
sees?

No,
for in
the moonlight
we
see him
shuffle
on,
and
with
a click
of the
claw
then
he's
gone,
oblivious
to the
scorn
heaped
upon.

And
when
the stage
is forever
empty
and
the sweet
dell
forever
bare,
will
there be
a
sign
that
says
"The English
Badger
once
lived
here."

*Note number 19

49. Boris The Buzzard

On a
clear
warm
summer
day,
across
the Cornish
moors,
flies
this bird
of prey.

On
rising
thermals
of air
he can
soar,
to
over
one thousand
feet
or
more.

Then
the earth
rises
up above
him,
in an
arc
of shadowed
green,
and fields
and hedges
take life
in this
world
of
in between.

And the
world
seems to
rock
and the
gigantic
roof
to sway,
as he
heads
towards
the cliffs,
and
the white
sea
salty spray.

And swirling
on thermals,
he dives,
twists
and turns,
and
paradise
is his,
above
the sea,
that chants
and churns.

Yet
then he
can be
vicious
when
his prey
he has
to capture,
for we
must
remember
he is
descended
from
the
velociraptor.

At sunset
he moves
like
a witch
and a broom
his outline
arresting
the gathering
gloom.

Then
he will
spread
his wings
to catch
the poor

field
mouse,
while
farmer
sits
by fire
in
solid
house.

And
as
evening
descends,
he takes
to his
rest
to guard
and protect
his eggs
and nest.

Then
high
on the
hill
against
the evening
sky,
the buzzard
will
sit
in majesty.
Bending
and preening
his

lithe silhouette,
his darkening
form
like a
shadow
marionette.

50. Mythica

*I had chosen to be born
into this granite barn
my soul had circled
the field and the farm
the rocks
and the stones
the barrows
and bones.*

*And here came I
with the bird in the snow
whose gentle whispering wings
showed me where to go,
that was the morn
of the ice cold sun
and as the stork departed
my life had begun.*

*I chose this hearth
on that silent
Christmas Eve,
where the spiralling spiders
web and weave,
across the beam
across
the eave.*

*I chose this land
with its crackling log fires
it's ancient energies
fogous and menhirs
chose the granite
and the ragged clothes
the cruel cold snow
pervading my nose.*

The place of Anna's birth

These lessons
of life
my karma
to be
the wheels
that turn
the soul's
journey.

Yet the gift
of the cold
morning dew,
were the diamonds
placed there
for me
and for you.

Yet
did we see
through
diaphanous
looking glass,
the emeralds
that
were placed
on the
long
waving grass.

Yet
did we know
on the
dancing
blue sea,
those
sapphires
were
placed

there
for you
and
for me?

And the stars
and the heavens
that softly
surround,
and the gentle
wind of sweetness
where
the buttercups abound
and the fox cubs
tumbling
with their
soft furry heads
and rabbits
running
to their burrows
and their
beds.

And now
my being
has a spirit
that calms,
as the moon
slips into
it's
westerly
arms.

No more dragons
to fight
no more fears
of the night

simple
resignation
of a gentle
kind,
and a soft
warm zephyr
to ease
my mind.

And
as I arrive
in that sacred place
my heart
explodes
with
humble grace.

And
the moving hand
still writes
but no longer
is it me,
I step aside
I close the door
I embrace
the
karmic sea.

Anna leaving the cottage at 17 years old

Au Revoir
Je Reviens
Anna

Note 1.

Lanyon Quoit

This Penwith Chamber Tomb may be dated c.3,200 - 2,500 BC from Neolithic Times.

This Penwith Chamber Tomb was originally much larger than it is today. Records show that a man mounted on horseback could ride underneath and through the Quoit. However, in the great storm of 1815, one of its granite legs was broken. This group of stones, was re-erected in 1824, and stands at the North end of a long barrow. The actual mound of the barrow (of which scant traces remain) lies N/S. It measures 90ft x 40ft.

The Quoit is a Dolmen composed of upright unhewn stones, roofed generally with a single huge stone. These roof stones are usually wedge-shaped. The primary intention of the Dolmen was to represent a dwelling place for the dead. It is believed that most, if not all the now exposed Dolmens were originally covered with a great mound of earth or smaller stones at the opposite end of the Lanyon Quoit barrow, other stones may indicate additional burial cists. Date c.3,200 - 2,500 BC.

The early Dolmen builders were in the Neolithic stage of culture. Their weapons were of polished stone.

Extracts from:

Celtic Myths and Legends by T. W. Rolleston. Studio Editions Ltd 1994.

In the

'Guide to Prehistoric England' by Nicholas Thomas 1960.

Lanyon Quoit is listed as: - a chambered long barrow. SW/430337. 2 miles SE of Morvah (B3306) on N side of Road to Madron and Penzance.

Note 2

Fern

The following two paragraphs are entries from 'Culpepper's Complete Herbal."

1) Fern (Brake or Bracken)- (Pteris Aquilina)

Description. - Of this there are two kinds principally to be treated of, viz. the male and the female.

Place. - They grow but too frequently upon commons and heaths.

Time. - They flower and seed at Midsummer.

Government and Virtues. - They are under the dominion of Mercury, both male and female.

2) Fern (Osmond Royal, or Water) - (Osmunda Regalis)

Description. - This is the biggest of our English Ferns.

Place. - It grows on moors, bogs, and watery places, in many parts of this country.

Time. - It is green all the summer, and the root only abides in winter.

Government and virtues. - Saturn owns the plant.

The following is an extract from Encyclopaedia Britannica.

'Ferns constitute an ancient division of vascular plants, some of them as old as the carboniferous period beginning about 358.9 million years ago., even before the dinosaurs.

These ferns were one of the first big plants to live on land, and helped make oxygen, which made the land ready for other life to start living too.

The illusive fern grows from spores which can travel tens of thousands of miles.

It is purported to have magical qualities and in Shakespeare's Henry IV, fairies were made invisible by the seed fern.

Also refer to the book by Thomas Moor 'The Ferns of Great Britain*.' This is a scientific description of all the variety of ferns found in Great Britain.

*See bibliography.

Note 3

Crow

The following is an extract from 'The Children's Encyclopaedia' by Arthur Mee.

"The crow family is, indeed, at the head of all the winged hierarchy. They are highest in mental development, the philosophers of the tribe; and, foremost in their ranks, science places the sagacious raven.

In these islands we have two species of Crow; the Carrion Crow and the Hooded Crow.

The head, throat, wings and tail of the Hooded Crow are black, the rest of the plumage is an ashy grey; whereas the Carrion Crow is entirely black, except for a greenish violet sheen, seen here and there.

The Crow and the Raven are both wise, cautious and self-reliant."

Note 4

Fairies of Madron Wishing Well

For many people the Celtic Baptistry and the Wishing Well at Madron, seem to hold magical qualities.

For me also, as I was born just across the fields from these two iconic entities, as were my brother and sister.

In researching the age of the Celtic Baptistry, the information which seems the most reliable, is, that it was built in the sixth Century, by St Maddern, who is reputed to have come from Brittany. He landed on the shores of Mounts Bay and followed the stream to its source, and there he built a baptistery.

Here he provided a place for Baptism and the water became famous for its healing qualities.

The Wishing Well itself is thought to be much older. Rory Te'Tigo, the West Cornish Antiquarian and Academic Sculptor suggested that it is likely to be of Phoenician origin. We are aware that the Phoenicians were highly skilled sea farers and that they did travel to Cornwall to trade for tin. It is very likely that they sought water on their travels, and that they found the location of the spring while enroute to the tin mines. Rory said that one main indicator is the rectangular shape of the well.

The following is an extract from "Charles Henderson: Notes on the 109 ancient parishes of the Four Western Hundreds of Cornwall (1910-24), published in the Journal of the Royal Institution of Cornwall, 1955-60.

"The separate well may once have been enclosed in a well-house," and Charles Henderson states that "there were formerly steps leading down to the well," however there have been many changes made to the chapel, well and stream over the centuries.

The following is an extract from Robert Hunt: Popular Romances of the West of England. London: Chatto and Windus 1923.

"It should be understood that there are in Cornwall five varieties of the fairy family.

1: The Small people

"The small people are believed by some to be the spirits of the people who inhabited Cornwall, many thousands of years ago."

2: The Spriggans

"The Spriggans are found only about the cairns, coits, or cromlechs, burrows or detached stones, with which it is unlucky for mortals to meddle."

A correspondent writes "This is known, that they were a remarkably mischievous and thievish tribe. It is usually considered that they are the ghosts of the giants, certainly, from many of their feats, we must suppose them to possess a giant's strength."

3. The Piskies or Pigseys

"This fairy is a most mischievous and very unsocial sprite. His favourite fun is to entice people into the bogs by appearing like the light from a cottage window, or as a man carrying a lantern."

4. The Knockers (or Buccas or Bockles)

"These are the SPRITES of the mines. They are said to be the souls of former workers of the tin-mines of Cornwall."

5. The Browney

"This spirit was purely of the household. Kindly and good, he devoted his every care to benefit the family with whom he had taken up his abode."

6. "In Cornwall another popular creed is that the fairies are Druids who are becoming smaller and smaller, because they will not give up their idolatries."

And should you venture to the Baptistery and the Wishing Well, do take care. Please respect this sacred place, so that it may bring a source of comfort both to you, and to our future generations.

And while you are there be on your guard, for just as there are both good and mischievous piskies, so there are both good and naughty fairies.

Note 5

The Hawthorn Tree

"The Hawthorn is very common in Britain, it's flowers, fruits and leaves all making it easily identified. It is also called the May Blossom, the fragrant blossom of the month of May.

The crimson berries which appear in the autumn, are so numerous at times as to give the impression of a crimson cloth. They are eaten as food in times of scarcity, in some lands, and peasants made from them a fermented drink.

Old books refer to them as "good for hogs."

In the winter, and especially the cold fierce months of January and February, the Hawthorn is stripped of all it's fragrant flowers and fruits and leaves and changes its character entirely to protect its survival from wind, snow and gales. It then becomes the spiky grey bush that bends and flexes it's bare cold branches, in order to survive the harsh cold winter."

Extracts from the Children's Encyclopaedia by Arthur Mee.

Note 6

St Michael's Mount

When I was a child, I would sit in the little granite window space and look down the fields to the Bay and St Michaels Mount. This was in the cottage where I was born. The granite walls were three-foot-deep and I could climb into the window space, pull the curtains behind me, and disappear into my dream world in my escape box.

St Michael's Mount always looked mystical and I suppose because so many people gaze on it with affection, it has embodied those qualities.

The Mount was once joined to the land by a narrow stretch of woodland. This land did in fact extend all the way to the Scilly Isles, and is known as the Lost Land of Lyonesse.

Legend tells us that the giant, Cormoran, built the Mount from grey and white rocks. When the giants were crashing about the land of Cornwall, the Mount was known as the White Rock in the Wood, or in Cornish "Carreg Luz en Kuz, or known as Grey Rock in the Wood "Karrek Loos yn Koos"

Geology suggests that rocky outcrops such as the Mount, have evolved, through billions of years of shifting continents, colossal restless ocean tides, and forces of nature.

Then as the Ice Age ended, the land around the Mount and the Scilly Isles became flooded.

This land had been the home of a people called the Silures.

On this land there had been thick forests, and at Penlee Museum in Penzance, there is a piece of oak taken from the sea floor, which is purported to be part of the old forest. This was donated to the museum by Stephen Bond.

St Michaels Mount was inhabited in Neolithic times. Sources of dates of this era vary considerably. In my research I have used information and details from a book called 'The Story of Prehistoric and Roman Britain.' By C. W. Airne, M.A.

In this book information and illustrations are reproduced by the Trustees of the British Museum.

This book states that the Neolithic Age started about ten thousand years ago i.e. 8,000 BC and lasted until 3,000BC. The Neolithic Age in Britain ended then, due to the invasion of races who had learnt how to work with and fashion metal. This took Britain into the Bronze Age.

Artefacts have been discovered on St Michael's Mount. These include pieces of flint and arrowheads. There is also evidence of early occupation there from the discovery of a round house settlement of the East side of the island, dating from Neolithic times.

One mystical legend about the Mount is that the Archangel Michael appeared there, before local fishermen in the 5th Centre A.D.

In the 11th Century A.D., St Michael's Mount was given to the Benedictine Religious Order of Mont St Michel, in Normandy, by Edward the Confessor.

In the 12th Century the monks of this sister isle built the church and the priory.

In 1193 the Mount was seized by Henry La Pomeray.

In 1473, during the War of the Roses, the Mount was occupied by the Earl of Oxford.

During the approach of the Spanish Armada, in 1588, a fire was lit on the church tower of St Michael's Mount, to warn London and England of the impending attack of the Armada.

In the English Civil War which started in 1642, the King's men defended the Mount against Oliver Cromwell's men.

Note 7

King Arthur and Excalibur

Lyonesse
A lost land said to have existed beyond Cornwall. Some thought it identical with Liones, the kingdom of Tristan's father, but this may originally have been Lothian Leoneis, later confused with a region of Brittany (Leonais). As to the lost land itself, a legend told that, when Arthur had fallen in his last battle, Mordred pursued the remnant of his army into Lyonesse. The ghost of Merlin appeared, the land sank and Mordred's forces were destroyed. Arthur's men, however, reached what are now known as the Isles of Scillies and survived. Did such a land exist? Readers of Tennyson may remember that he sets Arthur's final battle in Lyonesse.

Extract from 'The Illustrated Encyclopaedia of Arthurian Legends' by Ronan Coghlan, published by Claremont Books 1996. P165.

The following is an extract taken from "The Children's Encyclopaedia." By Arthur Mee. Published in 1908.

Speaking of King Arthur, Queen Guinevere and the Knights of the Round Table, Arthur Mee says "Historians incline to believe that the legend sprang from the true story of a Celtic Chieftain of the Fifth or Sixth Century, who beat off Saxon invaders, and made many other British Kings his vassals."

"In time it was arrayed in all the trappings of fourteenth-century chivalry and decorated and embroidered with magical jewels."

"In such a form it was written down in about 1469, by Sir Thomas Malory." He was the author of "Morte d'Arthur," which was printed by Caxton in 1485.

Guinevere was Arthur's wife. In a later story of the Arthurian legend, Guinevere was said to be the lover of Sir Lancelot. Lancelot was Arthur's trusted companion until he too, fell in love with Guinevere. Lancelot was a Knight of the Round Table.

Guinevere was the reason Arthur and Lancelot, went into battle against each other.

Tintagel Castle in Cornwall is said to be where Arthur was conceived. The Castle was rebuilt in Norman times so is not the original.

Arthur had two trustee horses, these were called Llamrei and Hengroen.

It is important to have faith and believe that those old English stories are based on true facts. We must remember that in those days the majority of the English population would have been illiterate, and there were few writers and no newspapers. Therefore, these stories would be passed down verbally; and possibly modified in the transition, but even so they are a vital part of our heritage.

In the book "Astrology and Kabbalah" by Z'er ben Shimon Halevi, he talks of the man who found the hidden buried city of Troy. People said it did not really exist, but he had faith and pursued his conviction. His name was Heinrich Schliemann.

He discovered the ancient city, which for him was proof that 'Legends are not just romantic fantasies.'

Note 8

The English Civil War

The fictious poem was inspired from reading about the Battle of Stratton, also known as the Battle of Stamford Hill; near Bude. This was a battle of the South-Western campaign and was fought on 16th May, 1643.

Cornwall was a Royalist stronghold and the Cornish were loyal supporters of King Charles I, against Oliver Cromwell. The Civil war waged from 22nd August 1642 until the 3rd September, 1651.

Under the command of the 1st Baron Ralph Hopton, The Royalist supporters marched from Bude to Stamford Hill, Stratton, and there ensued a terrible battle, that was fought until dusk. This time the Royalist managed to defeat the Parliamentarians.

'The King's Shilling' was an under-hand way of recruiting men to fight for the King.

The shilling would be dropped into the pewter tankard of a drinking man, who then, often slightly worse for wear, would be arrested. The next day he would have to appear in court, and because he was deemed to have accepted payment to fight, he would be 'railroaded' into joining the King's army.

Some men, however, accepted the recruitment without opposition, as average wages were really low at the time, and a shilling was considered to be a lot of money.

However, in the end Oliver Cromwell and the Parliamentarians defeated the Royalists, and King Charles I was tried for treason and executed in 1649.

Note 9

Mary Bryant

This poem was inspired by the remarkable true story of Mary Bryant, the young Cornish Highway woman from Fowey, who was born in May 1787.

The story has been told by 'Judith Cooke' in the book entitled 'To Brave Every Danger.' This is a detailed and fascinating account of Mary's life.

Note 10

Madron Workhouse

Records of Madron Workhouse go back to 1757. Then, there were large green gates at the entrance, and high walled gardens, where the residents grew vegetables. There was also a field where they kept pigs and cows and chickens.

In 1838, a new building was erected. This is believed to have been built by the French and American Prisoners of War. This is quite credible as there had been huge camps set up in Dartmoor for the prisoners.

The Workhouse overseers were renowned as being cruel and heartless. This ploy was used as a warning deterrent, in an attempt to stop folks entering through their doors.

The earliest records of workhouses in Britain, go back to the mid-sixteenth century.

Extract from 'Dandelions and Snails' by A.C. Miles-Smith.

Note 11

Goodnight my Darling Bessie

This poem is inspired by a true story. Into Madron Workhouse an old couple were admitted. They had worked all their lives and had managed to buy a small cottage by the sea.

However due to ill health they could no longer look after themselves, and the property, and were forced to enter the workhouse.

One of the main rules of Madron Workhouse was the enforced separation of husbands, wives and children.

Husbands were sent to one wing and wives and children to another.

Consequently, this couple were split up and could only see each other in the day.

My Mother's friend related how she would see them at breakfast, holding hands across the table and talking of what they would do when they eventually returned to their cottage.

Sadly, to say, they never returned and ended their days in the Workhouse.

Extract from 'Dandelions and Snails' by A.C. Miles-Smith.

Note 12

Ding Dong Mine

Mining in Cornwall began in the early Bronze Age, around 2,500 BC. Tin and Copper were the most common metals to be mined.

Also, to be mined were arsenic silver and zinc. Also, Kaolin was extracted.

In pre-historic times, the Phoenicians came to Cornwall to trade their riches in exchange for tin. That of course was in the years B.C. It wasn't until 55 B.C. that Julius Caesar and his army came to Cornwall to obtain tin and copper to make their armour.

Although some sources say that Ding Dong Mine was opened in the 17th Century, I think it feasible that Ding Dong Mine was operating in some form or other in the years B.C., as it is said to be one of the, or likely to be, the, oldest Tin mine in England.

Eventually in 1877, when tin prices fell to £41 per ton and very little tin ore was left, Ding Dong Mine ceased working and was closed down.

In its busiest days it had provided work for 500 people, in 1875, 265 people, but in 1877, only 64 people. Between 1850 to 1878 the output of tin was recorded at 3,472 tons, worth some £222,000.

The merchants, the bankers, the traders and speculators had grown rich and prospered, on the back-breaking work of the miners.

Note 13

The Ballad of Eliza Jane

I wrote this Ballad about the true story of Eliza Jane Hall, who started work at Ding Dong Mine, as a Bal Maiden, in 1873 at the age of 17.

She had only worked there for 3 ½ months, when she was caught in a terrible accident.

The Bal Maidens worked on the surface of the mine, sorting the ore. This had to be hammered with massive heavy hammers to extract the tin and copper. This was done in large frames. This was arduous and dangerous work as the women were constantly under threat of injury from flying debris. Hence they wore protective white hats called 'Gooks'.

Illness and sickness were rife, particularly with chest complaints and ailments such as diphtheria, tuberculosis, and bronchitis, due to the terrible conditions they worked and lived in.

Eliza's accident happened on the 8th July, 1873, at lunchtime.

The lunchbreak was nearly over when Eliza decided she wanted some fun. She was always larking around and decided that for a laugh she would climb onto the crown wheel of the whim.

"I will go round, I will go round" she had called, imagining herself to be on a fairground galloper.

However, as the lunchbreak had now ended, James Berriman, in the Engine House, was unaware that Eliza had jumped onto the rotating wheel. He heard a scream and stopped the engine.

Eliza's pinafore had got caught in the wheel, it had dragged her right leg in. This leg was crushed and her left leg was also severely mutilated. She died seven hours later.

She was rescued from obscurity in 2013 when the Madron Old Cornwall Society, erected a memorial stone to the memory of Eliza Jane Hall, in Gulval churchyard.

Note 14

Trengwainton House

This poem is based around a true story. Aunty Edmonds was not our real aunt, but a kind friend of my mother's who often made us children a nutritious snack before we walked home to Boswarthen from Madron.

Aunty Edmonds would recall the days of her youth, when she had worked as a scullery maid at Trengwainton House in Madron.

This beautiful old house was originally built in the sixteenth century and was acquired in 1867 by Thomas Simon Bolitho. It was left to Colonel Edward Bolitho in 1925, and the magnificent gardens given by him to the National Trust, in 1961 with provision made for the family to live there.

Aunty Edmonds was employed there in the late 1800's, when she was a young girl.

When balls and parties were imminent at the house, Aunty recalled, there was great bustling and excitement.

When all the work was finished, and the party was about to begin, Aunty and several other of the maids, would hide behind the bannisters, on the landing, and peeping through were able to see the proceedings through the large windows.

In those days there was a lake in front of Trengwainton House and the carriages and horses would parade around the lake, with their lanterns ablaze on the front of the coaches. They would have to wait their turn, and when the Butlers were ready, they could be announced, and able to proceed to the Ball.

Note 15

1800's – 1900's, **These Three** Cornish Painters

You will find details and stories about these painters in my book "Dandelions and Snail", A.C. Miles-Smith.

Note 16

Cheer Up Old Boy

The Battle of Britain - 10th July 1940 - 31st October.

A While ago I listened to a programme on the radio, where air pilots who had fought in the Battle of Britain, during the Second World War, were being interviewed. There were also recordings of the voices of those who, so sadly, had already passed away. These recordings were very sad, so I wrote a poem to honour their struggles. I marvelled at the genius of these unique men.

These war veterans were all about 90 to 100 years old They were all quick witted, clever, eloquent and selfless.

I gave the hero of the poem a Cornish name, in order to fit in with the theme of my poems. I thought I might eventually turn the poem into a song to honour the memory and the bravery of these men, with their razor-sharp minds who helped to win the war.

Note 17

Carbon to Carbon and Lamorna - The Woodcutters

The Woodcutters were originally formed in North Wales, after the Second World War. A group of men and their wives, all of the same philosophy of life, banded together to live in an old cottage in North Wales. There they originally worked for the Forestry Commission.

In the evenings, after work, they would sit around the fire and discuss politics, philosophy, ideologies and read from all the great thinkers and scholars of our times. They also loved to read from the great poets, T.S. Elliot, John Keats, Spenser, John Donne and Wordsworth. Some of these men were Quakers and consequently became conscientious objectors, as they 'did not believe in killing their fellow man.'

They lived just under the beautiful mountain of Cader-Idris, and often on their way to work would yodel, symbolising that the war had ended and they were free.

From North Wales the band moved down to Lamorna in Cornwall and there they lived on the cliffs. my parents who were part of the Woodcutters, actually slept under a caravan for a while. The Woodcutters moved from North Wales to Cornwall in 1947.

In Lamorna other artists, intellectuals and free thinkers, joined them.

Read more about the 'Woodcutters' in "Dandelions and Snails", A.C. Miles-Smith.

Note 18

Reynard the Fox

"The fox is an ancient Briton, and he was here at a period, long anterior to the mammoth's days."

(Edward Step "Animal Life of the British Isles).

However, despite the Hunting Act of 2004, this cruel sport still continues in England.

Note 19

Brock the Badger

The British beast – the Badger – has left his marks in place names such as Brockham, Brockenhurst, Brockley, Brockholes and many more.

In the old forests of Britain, the badger must have been a common beast.

"The modern-day culling of the Badger has not been a success – we cannot justify the massive slaughter of our Badger, and the cruel culling.

It has now been scientifically proven that most cattle contract the Bovine TB disease from other cattle.

Hopefully, for the Badger, another of our threatened ancient friends, there is good news. Badger culling is to be replaced by Badger vaccination."

Quote from "Rosie Woodroff" – Biologist – Radio 4.

Bibliography

Readers Digest Atlas of the World. Published by The Reader's Digest Association, Inc 1987.

C.W. Airne, M.A. The Story of Prehistoric and Roman Britain.

Edward Step. Animal Life of the British Isles. Published by Frederick Warne & Co. Ltd, 1942.

Nicholas Thomas. A Guide to Pre-historic England. Book Club Associates LONDON 1960.

The History Companion to British History, edited by Juliet Gardiner and Neil Wenborn. Collins and Brown 1995.

T. W. Rolleston. Celtic myths and legends. Studio Editions 1994.

Z'er ben Shimon Halevi. Astrology and Kabbalah. The Urania Trust 2000.

Arthur Mee. 'The Children's Encyclopaedia'. The Educational Book Company 1908.

Thomas Moore, edited by John Lindley. The Ferns of Great Britain. Published in 1855 by Bradbury and Evans.

Judith Cook: To Brave Every Danger. "The Epic Life of Mary Bryant of Fowey". Macmillan 1993.

Cheryl Straffon. Pagan Cornwall: Land of the Goddess. Meyn Mamvro Publications 1993. St Just.

G.C. Boase. Reminiscences of Penzance. Penzance Old Cornwall Society 1976.

Bob Acton: A View from Carn Galver. Mining trails in the Far South West. Landfall Publications 1993.

Melissa Hardie: Penzance. Penzance Town Council 2000.

Winston Graham: Poldark's Cornwall. Chapmans 1994.